AN ENTRY FOR THE
Stephen Leacock Award
FOR HUMOUR FOR
2022

Praise for Marcel Strigberger

For *Birth, Death and Other Trivialities*

"Marcel Strigberger is an irrepressible humorist with a story teller's flair for spinning a yarn with true (and hysterically funny) insights into the basics of human nature."

—*Midwest Book Review*

"Marcel Strigberger has produced an often-amusing collection of short reflections of such topics as health and happiness, religion and, of course, the law."

—*The Globe and Mail*

"This quickly paced book makes it entertaining and intriguing to contemplate life."

—*Matrimonial Affairs* (Canadian Bar Association, Family Law Section)

For *Poutine on the Orient Express*

"Get ready for a joyous journey filled with Marcel's wit + wisdom. You will be traveling many delightful miles with Marcel as your tour guide as he provides enlightening commentary with just the right light touch. When Marcel takes you along for the ride, you'll see that his mirth is universal—whether you spell it "humour" or "humor.""

—Dr. Joel Goodman
Founder/Director of The HUMOR Project, Inc.

"Marcel Strigberger's entertaining book brings thoughtful, insightful, twisted, and funny views to the travel experience. And from my personal point of view, that's what good humor is all about. Keep laughing!"

—Dave Schwensen, author of *How to Be a Working Comic*
Former talent coordinator for A&E's *An Evening at the Improv*

"There are lots of books about travel, and lots of funny books, but not many funny books about travel. In this book Toronto wit Strigberger is working at the top of his game."

—Mark Breslin, CEO and founder of Yuks Yuks

For *Boomers, Zoomers, and Other Oomers*

"This book is fantastic! I didn't stop reading it until the end. It's witty, insightful and engaging. It speaks to multiple generations."

—Jeremy Miller, author of *Sticky Branding*

"Marcel touches on the topic of aging with both humour and grace. He reminds us that if we can't laugh at ourselves at THIS age, we're definitely taking life too seriously. And really, age only matters if you're a grape. In which case, you're really wine. We all get better with age."

—Mona Andrei, author of *Superwoman: A Funny and Reflective Look at Single Motherhood*

"In reading Marcel's book, I felt like I was taking an enjoyable walk down memory lane with a knowledgeable guide. Most important, I got some great laughs too."

—Dr. Riley E. Moynes, author of *The Four Phases of Retirement*

"In our wisdom years we possess the ability and the luxury to see life through humor. Your book fulfills a real need."

—Dr. Zvi Lanir, author of *The Wisdom Years*

"If laughing is indeed good for your health, feel free to use not money to pay for *Boomers, Zoomers, and Other Oomers*, but your health card number. At the beginning of the pandemic we at *The Lawyer's Daily* asked funnyman/lawyer Marcel Strigberger: 'Forget for the moment the entire planet is depressed, unemployed, sick, frustrated, wheezing and maybe even facing the end of days. Would you be so kind as to make everybody laugh? Week after week?' Which is precisely what he did. This book is exhibit A."

—Peter Carter, Analysis Editor, *The Lawyer's Daily*

For humour (humor?) talents generally

"Strigberger is a comically gifted lawyer."

—*The Lawyers Weekly*

"Strigberger presents his material in his witty, stand-up comedy style."

—*Lifestyles*

"Strigberger's personality jumps off the page, with his humble humor and sharp wit."

—Blair Chavis, Assistant Managing Editor at the *ABA Journal*

Bless you all!

—Marcel Strigberger

MARCEL STRIGBERGER

Boomers, Zoomers,
and Other Oomers

A Boomer-biased Irreverent Perspective on Aging

marcelshumour.com

ISBN: 978-0-9959501-2-2 (print)
ISBN: 978-0-9959501-3-9 (ePub)

CONTENTS

ACKNOWLEDGEMENTS

Did you ever wonder whether writing a book can get lonely? It can and it does. I can take great comfort that I had a number of kind and competent people I was able to bother when I got tired talking to myself. This is as good a time and place as any to acknowledge some of these gracious souls.

Let me start with my editor, Andrea Lemieux. I was of the illusion for ages that we are all editors in that all it takes to get it right is to run the Word spell check. Illusion shattered. Andrea recrafted my manuscript knowing when to distinguish "could" from "can," "that" from "which," and numbering, such as "seven" from "7."

She also ably fact checked my comments along the way, noting errors I made such as thinking that Starbuck's largest coffee size was called "Grande." What can possibly leave anybody to come to that conclusion otherwise?

Most encouraging, Andrea told me that reading my manuscript often made her laugh out loud. I don't know. If an editor laughs out loud in the forest, does she make a sound? The mystery remains.

I also wish to thank and acknowledge people who were good enough to spend time reading my drafts or listening to my pleas, and who otherwise gave me sage feedback, much of which I followed.

Thanx Rene and Sam Geist for your suggestions on structure and content, including directing me to all those amusing quotes.

I also wish to acknowledge some able authors who are gurus on the subject of really enjoying life your way as you get older, when you no longer have to please a boss or your customers. They took time from their busy post-"retirement" time to read this book and provide me with their wisdom.

Thank you Dr. Riley E. Moynes (thefourphases.com), author of Canadian Bestseller, *The Four Phases of Retirement: What to Expect When You're Retiring.*

Thank you to Dr. Zvi Lanir, author of *The Wisdom Years: Unleashing Your Potential in Later Life.*

Writing a book is often the easy part. Marketing is a greater trick. To this end I am indebted to Jeremy Miller, a unique marketing genius, and author of *Sticky Branding: 12.5 Principles to Stand Out, Attract Customers, and Grow an Incredible Brand.*

I am also most grateful to Lisa Shiroff, who helped a technophobe like me try to understand or at least tolerate the e-world. Or is it i-world. She even proved to me that Amazon is actually reachable by telephone.

And hello, fellow humourist and country-lady from Montreal, Mona Andrei, author of *Superwoman: A Funny and Reflective Look at Single Motherhood.* Mona confirms that we can use humour in just about any situation.

Let me also mention Tsufit, author of *Step into the Spotlight! A Guide to Getting Noticed.* Her tips were invaluable. Her full name, however, is not out in the spotlight and it remains a mystery (something like that editor laughing out loud).

All these great books are available on Amazon, and at other fine retailers.

I am grateful to Peter Carter, Analysis Editor, *The Lawyer's Daily*, who kept me busy and in shape honing my craft by giving me the opportunity to pen a weekly column to lighten up the lives of lawyers, who, like the rest of us these times, can use some lightening up.

Finally, I want to thank my wife, Shoshana, and kids, Daniel, Natalie, and Gabriel, and their respective offspring, for providing reams of experiences and material for the content. They were also helpful in assisting me with tech matters, such as translating into English my discussions with associates at the Apple store.

Oh yes, thank you all, dear readers. We all share one major quality. Whether you call it time flying by or the clock ticking, since you started reading this page, you and I, without exception, have aged. And that's a good thing. We are now all on the same page.

Cheers.

INTRODUCTION

Hey, Boomers! Aging? You've already aged since you opened this book. We've got rapport. Let's have some fun together. It's all better than it looks.

I'll bet you think this is a good place for a quote from Charles Dickens. Agree. Here it is. The opening lines from *A Tale of Two Cities* speak volumes today.

"It was the best of times, it was the worst of times, it was the age of wisdom, it was the age of foolishness, it was the epoch of belief, it was the epoch of incredulity, it was the season of Light, it was the season of Darkness, it was the spring of hope, it was the winter of despair, we had everything before us, we had nothing before us, we were all going direct to Heaven, we were all going direct the other way."

You get the picture? Dickens couldn't make up his mind? Or just maybe it seems fitting, as we sit at home in the midst of the COVID-19 pandemic, trying to make some sense of the situation. Wear masks, don't wear them. It's a plague. It's a conspiracy. It was caused by bat soup. It was caused by a lab. Open up, lock down.

You get the feeling nobody has the answers? Is Dickens looking relevant now?

I suppose most of us have been hibernating this way as we are labelled as "high risk." And there are many of us on the planet. After all, we started sprouting in 1946 until about 1964. That's why we are called baby boomers. I say we are the bread and butter of all current generations, having experienced a range of excitement from the milkman delivering bottles in a horse and buggy, through the first moon landing to, most important, the invention of the sticky Post-it Notes. The younger generations are trying to figure out how to react to us. They don't even know what a milkman is.

There is certainly intergenerational conflict. We call the younger bunch "snowflakes" and "Peter Pan," suggesting they refuse to grow up and take responsibility. The latter blame us for the world's major issues, such as climate change, the economy, and large outstanding student loans. I don't know about other boomers, but I blame the millennials and Generations X and Z for supporting Starbucks' nomenclature of coffee sizes, calling them "Grande," "Venti," and "Trenta." Are they talking coffee, or Columbus's ships?

My view is that all of this skepticism and conflict is intrinsic—in our human DNA. It has really been going on forever. As Mark Twain put it over one hundred years ago, "When I was a boy of fourteen, my father was so ignorant I could hardly stand to have the old man around. But when I got to be twenty-one, I was astonished at how much the old man had learned in seven years." Sound familiar?

But this book is not meant to be a sociological treatise on current intergenerational conflict. No distracting footnotes or references to track down. When I hit age seventy, I decided to hang up my lawyer shingle after forty-plus years in the trenches and really have some fun looking at and writing about life from the perspective of our generation. And there is lots of fun to be had, from dealing with cashless banks, to negotiating timing issues with your prostate while driving, to listening to millennials trying to complete a sentence without uttering the expression "OMG."

I agree, seventy may or may not be the new fifty, but it certainly isn't the old seventy. Our health may not be perfect, but when we talk, unlike the millennials, we are actually able to say a phrase that does not end with a question mark. When asked what day it is today, we don't say "Tuesday?"

All good. And so, let's get on with it. As the Looney Tunes song goes, "On with the show this is it."

CHAPTER ONE

Quick Quiz: What Is Aging?
Shakespeare Says ...

You can't help getting older, but you don't have to get old.
~ George Burns

For me, three signs confirmed that I was aging: (1) when people started calling me "Mister Strigberger," (2) when I first came across doctors who were younger than I was, and (3) when I started asking people, "Do you remember *Gilligan's Island*?"

Regarding the Mister part, initially I would look around thinking they were addressing my dad. He was Mister. After all, like all dads he wore a fedora. A father hat. That's a Mister. I was Marcel.

As for doctors, when we were kids all doctors were elderly, sporting a grey three-piece suit, glasses, and an arrogant demeanor. You dare not stare one in the face or ask too many stupid questions, such as "will this hurt?" If you did, you risked his giving your parents that stern look, that doctor look, saying, "You know, I can do something about this brat."

Your parents would then beat their breasts and promise the good doctor it won't happen again, and that next time they would bind and gag the kid.

How times changed! One day, when in my thirties, I visited the children's hospital ER with my daughter. The doctor, who resembled a senior high schooler, wearing green scrubs with Bugs Bunny characters pasted on, introduced himself with "Hi, I'm Dr. Jimmy. What brings you here, Natalie?"

Yep, I was aging. *Gilligan's Island* needs no further comment. It speaks for itself.

When I think of aging, what comes to mind is Shakespeare's "Seven Ages of Man" from *As You Like It*. (Actually, when you get on in years you don't always like it.) No discussion about life flying by would be complete without mentioning this classic poetic monologue. Here's the excerpt. (Note for the millennials: One-minute read—sorry.)

All the world's a stage,
And all the men and women merely players;
They have their exits and their entrances,
And one man in his time plays many parts,
His acts being seven ages. At first the infant,
Mewling and puking in the nurse's arms;
And then the whining school-boy, with his satchel
And shining morning face, creeping like snail
Unwillingly to school. And then the lover,
Sighing like furnace, with a woeful ballad
Made to his mistress' eyebrow. Then a soldier,
Full of strange oaths and bearded like the pard,
Jealous in honour, sudden and quick in quarrel,
Seeking the bubble reputation
Even in the cannon's mouth. And then the justice,
In fair round belly with good capon lined,
With eyes severe and beard of formal cut,

Full of wise saws and modern instances;
And so he plays his part. The sixth age shifts
Into the lean and slippered pantaloon,
With spectacles on nose and pouch on side;
His youthful hose, well saved, a world too wide
For his shrunk shank; and his big manly voice,
Turning again toward childish treble, pipes
And whistles in his sound. Last scene of all,
That ends this strange eventful history,
Is second childishness and mere oblivion;
Sans teeth, sans eyes, sans taste, sans everything.

We'll see soon that not much has changed. Now the focus is more on different generational designations, such as baby boomer, Generation X, millennial, etcetera.

Actually, come to think of it, most of Shakespeare's stages, as he describes them, don't look too good. Firstly, the infant is totally helpless. I know what puking means but I had to look up "mewling." That translates as crying feebly or whimpering. Not off to a great start at all. Next?

The schoolboy does not look too happy at all. Actually, I never knew they had schools in the days of Shakespeare. I just presumed everyone grew up on a farm and milked cows and watched sheep all day. I guess some people lived in the big cities, like Stratford or London. And even if there were some schools, it's unlikely they were free. Most parents couldn't afford to send their kids to school. I suppose these lads didn't creep there unwillingly, like snails. They probably didn't even own a satchel.

The part about the lover looks bang on. I guess the reluctant schoolboy gets a little more motivated at this stage when he gazes at his mistress' eyebrow. That gets him sighing like a furnace. Hormones kick in you know. All of this still applies to today's youth. I can't confirm these guys do the ballad thing anymore. But having experienced this stage before (in the twentieth century), I will say, had I composed that woeful ballad to my mistress, it would not have been directed to her eyebrow.

As for the soldier, firstly, I grew up in Montreal. In Canada there is no mandatory military service so I cannot speak from personal experience. This stage likely encompasses ages eighteen into the thirties somewhere. The soldier thing may not apply bang on, but some of the other qualities might.

I'll admit I haven't come across too many youthful guys full of strange oaths. I can say, especially regarding my law practice, that I came across enough lawyers and clients who were jealous in honour, and sudden and quick in quarrel. Fortunately, dueling was banned in Canada until a while back. If it weren't, my law practice certainly would have taken a hit.

As for bearded like the pard, I actually sported a beard for over fifteen years in that soldier period. I wasn't sure what a pard was, so I Googled it too and it means "leopard." Makes sense. Shakespeare saved a syllable by taking a shortcut and calling it a pard. I imagine the "leo" part of it would apply to a lion. I never had a good look at a leopard to see what kind of beard he had.

As for the bubble reputation part of it, that still holds solid. Many folks risk their lives doing daredevil stunts like climbing dangerous mountains, going up in hot-air balloons, or eating poutine.

The next stage is the justice part. We are no doubt talking about judges. I think Shakespeare is off the mark on this one. The problem with this stage is that unlike the other stages, floating into the middle ages—forties, fifties, and so on—does not automatically lead to a position on the judicial bench. All infants puke and mewl. Most schoolboys creep to school unless they are transported there by school bus. Or carpool. And when you hit the teens, that furnace starts sighing. Agree?

And as I said, I am not sure about the soldier (no drafting in Canada you will recall). The bearded part, like the pard, sounds OK. But as for the judicial appointment—stage five, despite my passion for justice, no Ministers of Justice ever called me to announce my elevation to the bench. They appointed some questionable lawyers and left more deserving counsels like me in the trenches. Passing on me, they missed their chance. Does it bother me? Of course not. Shame on them.

That fair round belly was evident. The lawyers were too busy racking up those billable hours, not exercising, tied down to their desks, often on the phone, shouting those wise saws and modern instances. Or at least they thought they were wise. And I wouldn't blame the capons for those bellies. I'd point the finger at those cheeseburgers.

Stages six and seven are where it starts getting really scary. You go from fat belly to a lean and slippered pantaloon. Which means? Webster's Dictionary defines pantaloon as "a character in the commedia dell'arte that is usually a skinny old dotard who wears spectacles, slippers, and a tight-fitting combination of trousers and stockings."

After reading this information I started getting this recurring dream about walking into a Walmart and the greeter says to me, "OK, boomer, you'll find pantaloons in aisle seven."

I never bothered looking up the phrase "old dotard." No clue what it means, but I'm not a dirty old man.

That stage seven is nasty. It's the last scene. Second childishness, sans teeth, sans eyes, sans everything. I suppose the bard would've been a bit more optimistic if in the sixteenth century they would have had dentures.

You'll notice that Shakespeare ascribes these stages to women as well. He says, "All the world's a stage, And all the men and women merely players." However, he goes on to describe what happens to men only. Maybe that's a good thing. I doubt women would look too charming in those pantaloons.

Whatever. I don't think Shakespeare would subscribe to the opinion that seventy is the new fifty. Then again, what did he know? He never made it to this stage. He died at age fifty-two. The old fifty. No clue what his teeth were like.

What has really changed since? We are perhaps more focused on generation classification. Like I said, we boomers are the bread-and-butter stage of all current generations having experienced it all. Right now you're probably asking, what does Truman Capote say? Thought so.

Life is a moderately good play with a badly written third act.
~ Truman Capote

Then again, what does Truman Capote know? The third act has gotten better. We're still on this big stage and there are lots of us kicking ass. But the other oomers view us differently. You ask what other oomers call us? Ah hah!

CHAPTER TWO

What Do the Kids Call Us Boomers? You Ask. The Good, the Bad, and the "Whatever"

Age is not a particularly interesting subject. Anyone can get old.
All you have to do is live long enough.
~ Groucho Marx

A rose by any other name? There is a myriad of expressions the younger gang uses to describe older people or aging generally. Most don't smell like roses. They fall into three categories. The good, the bad, and the ugly.

Let me start with the good. Golden years. That's it. Short list. I can't come up with any others. Even this one is dubious, given Shakespeare's comment, "All that glitters is not gold." But we had better grab what we can. Gold is still better than silver, which is supposedly a metaphor for the colour of our hair.

You'll also hear people say that Henry lived to the "ripe" old age of ninety-three. That doesn't sound too bad except for the fact that Henry will never hear this comment, given that he has over-ripened and expired. He is past his best-before date.

Oh yes, and there is "senior," as in being over age sixty-five? But except for some of the perks that may come with this label, which perks I'll get to later, there is nothing flattering about being called a senior. It's not like having a military rank, where you can order people around. It would be nice if it were. The first thing I'd do is go over to millennials and their offspring and shout, "Attention! Attempt a virtual impossibility. Put your mobile phones down for a minute."

Then there is the bad and the ugly. I won't distinguish. I'll leave this to the ears of the beholder. Let me start with the latest buzzword: "OK boomer." This remark was made by some twenty-five-year-old MP in New Zealand to an older colleague during a parliamentary debate. He interrupted her and she said, "OK boomer." In short, this is meant to say, "Hey old man. Whatever you say, say it, as nobody really cares. You're over sixty-five, meaning your value and opinion is next in line to a dial phone. Your generation may have had some relevance in the 1960s and 1970s, but all this is now passé. I think that's a French word. Whatever. Your generation is responsible for all the evils of the world, including climate change, war, and our inability to get a job, whatever a job means. I think it involves work. OMG! Look what you've done to the world. You make me uncomfortable—I need a break. Give me space to have some avocado and kale." I think that describes it.

Let's discuss some less flattering phrases that get lobbed at us. Like old fart. The perpetrators of this expression presume that only those over sixty-five engage in flatulence. Or should I say farting. Some of them may not even know what the word flatulence means.

They really age us when they call us a dinosaur. Given that there are no dinosaurs in existence anymore, this expression suggests we don't even exist. At best, we are a relic, or maybe a fossil. And while we're on the letter *F*, I'll throw in the *F*-word: old "fogey." Though the term is used to describe someone overly conservative and old fashioned, in the early 1800s it was used to describe an invalid or a wounded soldier. It actually derives from the French word *fougueux*, meaning "fierce" or "fiery." I'll bet none of you young pishers ever knew this. Why don't you run it by Siri?

While we're into foreign phrases, let's not forget the Yiddish *alter kakker* or *alter pisher*. You don't need Webster's Dictionary to figure these out. You can guess what those expressions mean.

Did I mention "geezer"? Fortunately, that sounds like "geyser," which at Yellowstone Park is also called "Old Faithful." We deliver.

There are even some derogatory terms that are gender specific. These for a man include "Pops," "old-timer," and "old goat." The latter is attributed to older men who show an interest in women. At least these old goats when they are with a woman, unlike many millennials, are focused, not clutching a cellphone. And the old goat certainly isn't kaput. And unlike dinosaurs, goats are still in existence.

As for "old dotard," like I said before, if your curiosity is peaked, you guys can Google that one.

Women do not escape the derogatory expressions, often being called "biddy," "old bag," or even worse if the lady's mental faculties are being assailed, "old bat."

I'll admit that in many ways we may be quaint, passé, or over the hill. But at least we put on our boots, rolled up our sleeves, and climbed that hill. And from the top we got a great view of what's in front of us and what's behind us. And if we wish to do so, we can indeed go into the pasture and enjoy the experience.

Other Oomers' Lingo

"When I use a word," Humpty Dumpty said in rather a scornful tone,
"it means just what I choose it to mean—neither more nor less."
~ Lewis Carroll, *Through the Looking Glass*

In addition to words they use to describe us, the younger generations today seem to have a language of their own. I guess they always have had. Being a baby boomer, however, I have already forgotten the idioms of our youth. One reason for this amnesia no doubt is that we baby boomers are too busy trying to remember all those pin numbers we need to get us through the day. We are too busy trying to focus on how to set our home alarms, retrieve our telephone messages, check our lab results online, and so on.

The lingo the kids use is not quite a whole language. It just involves a few phrases here and there, but it is quite distinct. I recall my millennial daughter's friend leaving a voice mail message on our line as follows. "Hi Natalie. Like it's me. It's one o'clock like but that's OK. Like you can call me back tomorrow."

I am paraphrasing. In reality there were at least three or four more likes in that message. My daughter of course could readily equal her friend or the rest of the gang with those likes. She'd approach me and say, "Hey dad, like we have an exam next week in nuclear physics. Like I'm not certain about the part about splitting the atom. Can you help me?"

She came to the right place. At least she thought I was still important.

It got me thinking though. Why do they use the word "like"? When I last checked Webster's Dictionary, "like" was defined as either a verb meaning to love or appreciate something, or as a simile, as in it tastes like chicken. The kids have added a new dimension to the word, making it a filler of a sort. Or should I say, "like making it a filler."

Then I notice there is also a greeting they use. I am used to hearing something like "hi," "how do you do," or even "hello." My lawyer son greets his friends with the greeting, "Hey." The recipient of this greeting usually answers in kind with his or her "hey." Then along comes another chum and the two of them shout out to him, "Hey." The chum grunts back, "Hey."

Hello has another meaning these days. It is more derogatory. If someone does not see the obviousness in your argument, you say to him, "Hello?" This is seen when you want to speak with your kids on the phone and they respond quizzically, saying, "Hello? Can you just text me?"

This hello usually means, "Hey, which part of texting don't you understand? How do you expect us to communicate if you just don't get what's happening in the world?" This often gets followed by an OMG. And the "hey" in that sentence is the traditional hey, meaning "by the way."

My younger millennial son, Gabriel, still uses a word that I mentioned earlier, and that is very convenient. It answers many questions—other than the one I might be asking. I'll ask him, "Gabriel, did you see my Costco magazine?" He'll respond, "Whatever." I notice he and his colleagues use that one a lot. It's almost as if I am now supposed to respond, "Oh yes, of course, it's in the den under the sofa cushion. Thank you."

I wonder whether that word can get the kids through a school exam. It would certainly be nice if on a history exam a question appeared asking, "Who was Napoleon?" and you can get away with replying, "Whatever." Or perhaps to be more accurate, "Whoever."

After all, the kids presumably know the answer anyway. Why bother them for the details?

My favourite expression is the term used when there are problems. Or perhaps challenges. There is a word used covering all these contingencies. I overheard my young neighbour say, "I have to speak to my boyfriend about why he didn't get me flowers for Valentine's Day. He probably has a few "issues."

For the uninitiated, an issue is not an edition of a magazine, like the Costco one I could not find earlier on as it was located "wherever." "Issues" goes beyond problems. An issue denotes an entire psychological makeup explaining the behaviour of the culprit who has one. You use that term, and you sound knowledgeable. If for example you want to make a worthwhile comment about why Josef Stalin annihilated millions of his citizens, just say in passing, "Stalin had issues." All listening to you will nod affirmatively, take a puff on their pipes, and say, "Of course, that's it." Or should I say these days in Canada, a toke on their joint?

Bless them all. And what do we learn from all of this? Whatever.

But the aging, life cycle process moves along, hitting us all. Where are we going? It helps to know where we have been. I believe we can all enhance our lives by reviewing a little history. And our history is solid. Let me work backwards, going from older generations to younger. There will be no mention of any mewling and puking infants. Nor need there be. Nor will there be further mention of Truman Capote. Too pessimistic!

CHAPTER THREE

Boomers, Zoomers, and Other Oomers

Today is the oldest you've ever been,
and the youngest you'll ever be again. Yikes!
~ Eleanor Roosevelt

A ctually, she said those words—other than the "yikes."
Before I get into my current boomer generation, let me
pay homage to the elders (the real ones of course!). Age before beauty.

Pre-1945: The Traditionalists

The oldest is the group born before 1945. They are known as the
"silent generation." My guess for this designation is that many of these
good people are also hearing impaired, becoming this way as their
eardrums were blasted by the loud and crazy rock music of the later
generations. It often doesn't take much more than a passing car with
volume set to high bass, playing the best of Mick Jagger screaming,
to bring about sudden deafness.

This group is also known as "traditionalists." They worked hard,
respected king and country, and if they heard your school principal
punished you with the strap, after you eloquently explained your

innocence, they would add to the sentence. So much for the legal doctrine of double jeopardy.

They were never overprotective, allowing you to go out and play street hockey, on the street. If the team you were on lost the game, you would not come home with your tail between your legs and mope, bleating "not fair." And if you did, your mom would not rush out and suspect psychological trauma and drag you to a shrink. You learned quickly that in life there are actually winners and losers. The only ones who never seemed to lose were the Montreal Canadiens of the 1950s, who just about won the Stanley Cup every year. I doubt the mothers of the Toronto Maple Leafs rushed to console their sons.

I will say that the men were sexist. They would remove or tip their hats when encountering a lady, or hold a door open for her. They also had the gumption to call a woman "Miss" or "Mrs." The term "Ms." was still a term of the future, like "Apple."

Many had the pleasure of owning a mom-and-pop corner store, where neighbours and others would do their basic shopping. They would work long hours running the place, greeting you with a sincere smile and a hello. I suppose Walmart is similar in that it still carries on the greeting part. (I do hope now that I mentioned Walmart again that I don't have another episode of that recurring pantaloon dream tonight.)

Those stores in my Montreal neighbourhood also had delivery service. You made your food order and it would arrive later in the day via a teenager pedalling a bicycle. I'd say this service was even more efficient than Amazon. Nobody stole it off your doorstep. And if there were an error, you'd call Mom or Pop. And they would fix it without your having to listen to a voicemail telling you your call was important to them. It just was.

This generation spawned some great hockey players, namely Gordie Howe and Bobby Hull. Of course there were other players, but I single out these two as their greatness extended outside of the game in that they were known not to leave the arena until they signed their autograph for any kid hanging around with his or her writing pad eagerly waiting ringside for their hockey hero. They did not concern themselves with trivial matters such as payment as a result of bureaucratic and mercenary protocol that became commonplace down the road. They never had to tell a kid, nor would they likely have told him, "You can get my autograph via NHL.com/autographs/hey-kid-must-pay."

I had the joy over sixty years ago of being one of these kids, scrambling down the rows at the old Montreal Forum, notebook and pencil in hand, to join a crowd of kids at rink-side, where Gordie Howe was busy graciously accommodating his captivated young audience.

Why is it I remember with total clarity, after sixty years, those few moments with the man than I do his scoring records?

But the silent generation had one weakness. It generated a certain king: Elvis Presley. That was actually a good thing. His popularity as a singer was a bell-weather for perhaps the most popular singing group ever, the Beatles. I'll have more to say about them shortly. Elvis actually added sexual connotations with his performances. I recall when he appeared on *The Ed Sullivan Show* in the mid-fifties, the camera had to pan on his upper body so that the television audience did not see the King's hips swivel. No doubt that would be too much for the screaming female teenagers. Thank you, thank you very much.

Sex was to be confined to the bedroom. If you were lonesome tonight or lonely tonight, you were not going to get any suggestions on television. Uh huh huh!

We were now heading into the 1960s, and in my baby-boomer opinion this was the decade that was. And it was the baby-boomer generation that put its face on it. I'd say we started it all, and we were the major forerunners of what we have today.

1945–1964: The Baby Boomers—That's Us

What can we say about our group? Referring to the Stratford bard's chart, I'd say that while the traditionalists would now be in stage seven, we boomers are definitely in stages five and six. As the seventeenth-century philosopher René Descartes might have put it, "I have all my teeth, therefore I am."

Baby boomers started the modern age, being the transition generation, the link between the space age and the horse-and-buggy age. Literally. I recall back in my 1950s working-class neighbourhood in Montreal, not all residents had fridges. Ice boxes were not uncommon. And with them came the iceman, lugging large blocks of ice on a horse-drawn wagon. He'd amble along the quiet street shouting, "Ice, ice, ehhh!" I can understand the ice part, but like you I have no clue what the ehhh was about. First time I heard it I thought his horse dropped an equine deposit on the street.

We would often run out, and while the iceman was delivering a large block we'd snatch some loose shavings of ice from his wagon and munch them like popsicles. We would even feed some to the horse. The ice guy, when he came out, would chase us away, shouting, "Go 'way. Nehhh!" (Not sure if nehhh somewhat corresponded to ehhh.) His horse, however, had no problem with us.

Of note is that our parents had no issues with our nibbling on those not 100% questionably sanitary ice chips. Nobody asked us whether the iceman put on latex gloves. Fast forward sixty years later, when you visit a Costco that provides an array of food samples offered in paper wrappers sitting on a tray. (Remember those pre-pandemic days?)

I once pointed to an olive, and the server, thinking I had actually touched the wrapper, immediately picked it up like it was a dead cockroach and tossed it out. A couple of young bystanders behind me nodded her action with approval. I'm sure they assessed the situation carefully and likely concluded that the server had just averted the spread of the plague. And yet that, of course, still came around: COVID-19. Not my fault. I don't know as I write when the next time we'll see olives at Costco outside of their jar.

Baby boomers were also the first to transition from radio to television. For about fifty years people were happy with going auditory only, getting their news and entertainment fix compliments of Guglielmo Marconi's great invention, the radio. Suddenly in the 1950s, television became mainstream, and unlike our parents we grew up expecting not only to hear that the Montreal Canadiens scored a goal, but also to see Maurice "Rocket" Richard being congratulated by his teammates yet again for breaking record after record.

But the great Rocket wasn't wearing his red, white, and blue uniform. He, like all the other players, was visible in black and white only. Colour television was not prevalent yet. But we were grateful. At least we could keep the play-by-play announcers honest. The worst part about it all was our parents' comments like, "You kids are fortunate. When we were kids we were happy to gather around the family radio for entertainment. You're all spoiled." I'd say this older generation was weird. They just weren't with it.

But the television wasn't all wine and roses. It came with a problem: the rabbit ears antenna. Unless your structure had one of those roof antennae, very often your reception went on the fritz, usually when what you were watching was reaching a climax. For me, this inevitably was as Rocket Richard was rushing to the opposing net on a breakaway. You'd have to jump up and fiddle with those ears in the futile hope of restoring reception quickly. This would happen after a couple of minutes of antenna massaging with alternating utterings of expletives. By then the play, of course, was history. And in those days there was no instant replay. You missed it, you missed it. Life was cruel.

I was thinking. It would have been nice for the Rocket, as he started his moves, to think about his television fans cheering him on and maybe pausing, knowing we were trying frantically to perform antenna CPR. He never did. I guess this was his shortcoming.

The reception, of course, never went bonkers during a television commercial. You'd have to bear through some guy in a brush cut and suit touting cigarettes, reminding us next time we go to the store to remember to say "Players please." Nothing could interrupt this commercial, not even yanking those rabbit ears.

The 1960s: Exciting Times without Smartphones

The 1960s in my view was the decade that was. The citadel of tradition started to crumble. It all started with the election of President John Kennedy in 1960.

Kennedy right off the bat signalled a change in that at his inauguration he did not wear a fedora, or for that matter, any hat. This was the beginning of the end for the standard men's lid issue. The citadel suffered a further breach. The boomers took notice and moved forward.

Then came 1963 and the Beatles. Until then guys generally had short- to medium-length hair, combed, and often drowned in a bucket of hair greases, like Brylcreem. The commercial did say "Brylcreem, a little dab'll do ya." But it never did do ya. The alternative was that brush cut. I suppose your choice might in part depend on the local street gang you wanted to join.

The Beatles descended upon the scene like a tsunami, making their first major world appearance on *The Ed Sullivan Show*. Popularity wise, they were often described as Elvis, multiplied by four. Their mop-style hair caught on like a brushfire and suddenly every male just let his hair grow. No doubt barbers' business suffered a cataclysmic hit. Baby boomers were not cutting their hair anymore. As a salvage attempt procedure, many barbers changed their designation from "barber" to "hair stylist." Not sure if that helped. That's like Kentucky Fried Chicken calling their fried chicken "egg based."

My father, like all traditionalists, would of course get his hair cut regularly, commenting that the wait times at the barber were pleasantly reduced. He also had comments about the kids nowadays who thought they were smart letting their hair grow down to their tuchis like the Beatles. He predicted this long-hair fad, along with the Beatles, would fizzle out soon. (I never suggested traditionalists were great at predicting the future.) The citadel was starting to crash.

The 1960s were the years of revolution, the decade that was. With long hair came the hippies. And all that free love, and Woodstock. Yes, you subsequent generations, these players were the boomers. Yes, millennials, we were actually able to have sex without a smartphone in one hand. I know you don't believe that but it's true. Knowing that this would be a major challenge for you, I don't suggest you try that at home. I know well enough to toss in this disclaimer, absolving myself from any and all claims for damages suffered if you do attempt this feat. The disclaimer also applies in the event that you guys engage in sex while trying not to wear a Bluetooth earpiece.

The 1960s also experienced the Vietnam War. It was the boomers who established and led the anti-war protests. And many Americans were stationed in Canada, though not by Uncle Sam's command. These were the draft dodgers. I imagine these guys departed from Shakespeare's fourth stage in that they shunned being "the soldier." They were still nonetheless often full of strange oaths and bearded like the pard, jealous in honour, sudden and quick in quarrel. It seems these qualities at this stage are universal and perennial.

Those hippies often looked different than the pard, with their long hair. As well I can say that the pard likely took more baths. Then again, Shakespeare also had long hair. I can't say much about his bathing practices. I can probably Google it, but does anybody really care?

And Canada was not that exciting a world-class country until 1967, when Montreal hosted the world-class world's fair, Expo '67. For six months millions of visitors descended upon my hometown city visiting pavilions sponsored by over one hundred countries. It was common daily to see car convoys carrying kings and queens, presidents, and prime ministers. We boomers were there, making up the mainstay of the fair's employees. Suddenly, finding that elusive summer job became a piece of cake for all of us.

I say elusive as boomers had a solid work ethic, looking high and low to find a summer job both as a source of income and to keep us out of mischief. I spent one summer in the Laurentian Mountains working at a local village bowling alley as a pinboy. Gen Xers and millennials have no idea what that is. No, I did not say "pin up" boy. You see automatic pin setters were not prevalent until the late 1950s. As the pins did not just reset themselves after some hotshot bowler rolled a strike, they needed live people to reset them. The position came with some danger as too often the eager bowler could not wait for us to set up all ten pins and he would lob his ball full force down the lane. We'd have to jump to the side to save our skin. At that point, the pinboys would usually wave their fists at the would-be assassin, shouting a few oaths. And they were commonplace oaths, not strange at all. And for this job we got paid the grand total of 10 cents per player per string or game.

Salaries at Expo '67 were unreal. You got $2.50/hour to take tickets, sell guidebooks, or pick up trash. Much of that trash consisted of discarded tickets and guidebooks. I suppose the picker-upper was engaging in a form of recycling.

We didn't have to backpack it that year in order to see the world. The world came to us.

And speaking of Expo, we boomers were there a year or so later when the Montreal Expos opened their first major-league game. The games were played in a small open-air bush-league stadium called Jarry Park.

Our parents didn't have the pleasure of getting taken out to the ballgame—major league that is. And the subsequent generations grew up with the expectation when a few clouds appeared overhead to see a gargantuan roof suddenly roll over the arena. Actually, the team moved on to the Olympic Stadium in the mid-70s, where spectators were protected from the raindrops by a fixed gargantuan roof.

Unfortunately though, they were not protected from the roof itself as the place had a checkered history, having to be shut down on and off given small mishaps such as gargantuan pieces of roof crashing down.

And let us not forget perhaps one of the most significant events of the 1960s, if not of the century. I speak of the July 20, 1969, moon landing. We boomers were there front and centre seeing it happen. We remember it as though it just happened yesterday. We saw that small step for man, giant step for mankind unfold on our televisions. OK, they were black and white. At least mine still was. But it didn't matter. The moon landscape doesn't exactly resemble a peacock. And the moon is not made of blue cheese.

The world stretching back to the days of Adam and Eve has been fascinated by Mr. Moon. But the scientists unravelled all the mysteries in our days, for us. Of course, NASA used the latest technology to get it all done. Computers. My point is, our parents never dreamt of computers, whereas we boomers got our feet wet, noting that these artificially intellectual giants were indeed gigantic machines located in select exclusive organizations such as the government, and taking up a whole room. We knew they were out there. We also knew they were powerful and not always to be trusted as we all saw the in the 1960s movie *2001: A Space Odyssey*. To this day I avoid shaking hands with anyone called Hal. And for sure if I ever check into a motel and the desk clerk is called Hal, regardless of whether there is a Bates there or not, I ain't stepping into the shower. But at the time we never expected the birth of personal computers that can be worn on your wrist.

And let us not forget that the 1960s saw the rise of the women's liberation movement. Women's lib. As boomers we grew up with the notion that whereas boys can enter any occupation they desired, girls can aspire to grow up and become teachers or nurses. Sure, there were exceptions, but these were the common defaults.

I can say with certainty that in the 1950s I never came across a male nurse. All nurses were women, wearing white frocks and those little two-pointed white hats that resembled an envelope.

Trousers on women in the workplace was unknown. Women, as we boomers were aging up, wore skirts or dresses. Not that the men had it perfect. Remember, until the 1960s men had to wear those father hats.

And it's not as if boomer males had zillions of careers to choose from. Of course the classical professions were there front and center. I talk of law, accounting, engineering, and medicine of course, the latter if you could stand the sight of blood and guts and had this inexplicable obsession about keeping people waiting for ages to see you.

Then there were the trades. Interesting why Shakespeare names stage four as the soldier. I suppose more men enlisted in the army in his days than became tradesmen. It would not have had that same cadence and flow had he said, "And then the barber, full of strange oaths, seeking the bubble reputation even into the comb's teeth." As well, those strange oaths would probably come from his customers, who'd get upset after he nicked them with his razor. Certainly after a shave they would not be bearded like the pard.

But leaving the barbershop, women were still the "weaker gender." There was even a law in Quebec that contracts were not enforceable against infants, lunatics, and married women. That would not necessarily always be a bad thing as I could get my wife to sign those onerous contracts with my telephone providers. And anytime she would download some app or system where you consent to Apple or Adobe or Google to take over your first born by hitting "I agree," I'd take comfort in the fact that it would not be enforceable. Or as film-studio mogul Louis Mayer said, it would not be worth the paper it's written on.

And speaking of the law, almost all judges were men. The Superior Court judges were addressed as "My Lord." When the sporadic female justice reached the bench, this changed to "Milady." We lawyers at times found it awkward as we were not sure whether we had to bow or curtsy. But the trend to appoint more women to the bench took off with our generation.

And further speaking of the law, the 1960s saw the advent of lawyer and consumer-protection activist Ralph Nader. He took on mega corporations such as Ford and General Motors, calling out inherent defects in his book *Unsafe at Any Speed*. Ford Pintos, you might recall, had a little problem. Unlike their namesake horses, the pintos, the Ford Pinto, if involved in a collision, had a propensity to explode. That of course could be a problem, causing some unsavoury traffic delays.

Ralph Nader was not a baby boomer, being born in 1935. However, he flourished in the 1960s as this is when the season was ripe for dissent and change. And the baby boomers were there to listen to his inspirational words and to carry the torch and line up with him. We agreed a car manufacturer should design a car that when it hits another car, both drivers should be able to get out and exchange information, after maybe shouting at one another. Ford or other car manufacturers were not infallible. It was OK to tell them that the accident scene should not look like a snapshot of Pompeii.

And speaking of smoke, we did have one big vice. Smoking. It was OK to smoke. Many of our parents smoked. Non-smoking areas in public places were unheard of. This included hospitals. I once had concerns about the results of a chest X-ray as it showed some shadow. I was referred to the head of radiology at a large hospital for some follow up. The radiologist in chief, a sub-specialist in lung imaging, was informative, holding up my X-ray image against a light and explaining what it showed, all this while dangling a lit cigarette from his lips. Fortunately, I was OK. I did not complain to him about some of the ashes falling on my shoe. Nor did I ask if the hospital had a no-smoking zone.

Smoking was a virtual status symbol in those days. There were no age restrictions. You just had to show up at your corner store with about 35 cents and say, "Players please." (The commercial worked.)

It was as we got older and had our own kids that we realized and accepted that smoking can be hazardous, and we started leading the crusade against it. And as the saying goes, "Be careful what you wish for." Now we have legalized pot. I'll be bold enough to suggest smoking same is not appreciated by your lungs. Just as bad, or worse—cigarettes did not make you high while driving a car. Then again, people are responsible. Aren't they?

We boomers saw it all happen, from the ice age, or rather, the iceman age, to the moon landing. I can also add watching miniskirts, a creature of the 1960s, but someone may suggest this might be sexist, so I won't mention it. Cher by the way does refer to it in her song "The beat goes on." That is Cher the boomer.

The 1960s saw the ageless citadel breach, crumble, and crash. As Shakespeare might say, "Exit, baby boomers' stage."

All the Other Oomers: Gen Xers, Millennials, and Zoomers

Gen X, as it is called, includes kids born between 1965 and 1976. Its members as I write would therefore be between forty-five and fifty-six years old. Millennials run from the late 1970s to the late 1990s, and zoomers follow. As boomers, we don't really care what they all call themselves. What do they know? They never even came face to face with a black rotary dial phone. Also they screwed up their nomenclature. What letter follows Z? Looks as though they have now painted themselves into a corner.

Given that boomers were generated only as of 1946, for the most part we cannot claim credit for the segment of Xers born at the early end of the spectrum. At that point, using Shakespeare's frame of reference, we were somewhere in the lover and soldier stages. Since I was born in 1947, to have a kid born in 1965 would mean I would have to get working at around age seventeen. This was doable, but most of my contemporaries only talked about this work, or rather the pleasure I suppose. As they say, those who can, do, and those who can't, teach. Or in this case, those who couldn't, talked.

Now to create these Xers, first came marriage. Common-law cohabitation relationships were out there but not so common. Until well into the 1970s, unmarried partners had little or no property rights in the other's stuff. Nor did their children. I won't go into the details, but if your dad was not married to your mom and he died without a will, you got nothing. And if your dad married another woman, resulting in your having a half-sister, your wicked half-sister got your share. Nasty!

And if you intended to get married soon but you were already married and separated, and your new fiancée was a little bit pregnant, you wanted to get a final divorce decree pronto. The sentiment was that the kid should be born under the holy canopy of marriage. The *Divorce Act* (Canada that is) then had a two-stage process for getting out. First was the "decree nisi." This was a court order that said you are divorced, *but* you cannot remarry until you get past stage two, which was a "decree absolute." You had to wait at least thirty days to get this coveted decree.

However, there was a provision in the *Divorce Act* where the judge granting the decree nisi could dispense with the thirty days if the anxious couple could convince the judge that there was a Generation X bun in the oven that was not going to wait much longer and that His Honour would advance the course of justice as basically it was in the public interest to fast-track the final decree. Who ever said the law is an ass?

Things changed, of course, with time. The point is, once again we boomers were the link pin, experiencing the dark ages and the Renaissance, where the law said hey, a son is a son, a daughter is a daughter. The law no longer concerned itself with hanky-panky.

Again, whoever said the law is an ass? (OK, more Charles Dickens.)

Boomers got married much earlier than the Gen Xers going forward. I got married at age twenty-three, being a typical age for nuptials. I had my concerns and fears of course. Going back to Shakespeare, I felt a little like that whining schoolboy, creeping like snail unwillingly to the altar. I say this fifty years later, still married (to the same woman). And fortunately I don't wear a lean and slippered pantaloon. Maybe there is some wisdom in the expression "The seventies are the new fifties."

Then came the baby-boomer babies, those Xers. And there was one thing babies needed more than anything. I'm not talking love. Or milk. I'm talking diapers. For centuries a baby and a diaper went together like that proverbial love and marriage, which went together like that proverbial horse and carriage. But this too changed around the time we started having kids.

What was that change? you ask. No, it's not that our babies, Gen Xers, were born toilet trained. This group often acts as though they were endowed with super skills and talents, making them superior to their parents. But they did not come toilet trained, or so to speak, *prêt-à-potty*.

The 1970s saw the disappearance of cloth diapers, for all intents and purposes. Until then, parents had a choice of either washing cloth diapers or using a diaper service, which delivered a fresh stash weekly, or whatever, removing the soiled versions that you gingerly dropped into some mystical white container, closing the lid very quickly. The service drivers I recall drove white vans and wore white uniforms.

The 1970s saw the emergence of the disposable diaper. The word "Pampers" entered the lexicon. I'm not sure about the economics of one over the other. I know the environment wasn't the main topic of conversation.

And if you were out with your infant at a park, say, and he or she needed a diaper change, if you realized you forgot to bring along your own, you'd go over to another parent and ask if they could lend you one. It was like asking for a cigarette.

Actually, "lend" would be a misnomer as it would be most likely you would default on this loan. It would have made more sense to ask if they could just donate a Pamper. "I see you have a baby. Isn't she cute! Can you spare a Pamper please?"

You hoped that this parent used Pampers and not that diaper service. Otherwise I would not hold out on your lucking out and having that guy in the white uniform just show up at the scene like the Man from Glad.

Gen-X Kids Getting to School on Their Own? Perish the Thought

Another routine entered our lives. As these kids grew up a little and started attending pre-school, a new animal came into the picture. The carpool. Assuming that proverbial school bus was not an option, parents everywhere organized carpools, taking turns to ferry their kids to school.

The vehicle of choice for this mode of transportation was the station wagon. It was larger than a sedan and could accommodate more passengers, especially if it had an extra bench at the back, usually facing the rear, as did our 1985 Chevrolet Celebrity.

These vehicles were very versatile as many trades and other people would use them for commercial purposes. Sometimes in fact the owners would forget to clear the car for the transition from commercial to carpool, and this act of neglect would come to the attention of the parent driving when one of the kids would say "look what I found," waving around a hydraulic drill.

We of course put safety first, at least the safety of the day. Seatbelts consisted initially of only lap belts—shoulder belts being introduced later on. And use of whatever was there, or not, was not yet mandatory. The young passengers were small, and it made sense to pack them in economically. They didn't complain and beseech you to strap them in. They were happy having freedom of movement. This freedom generally enabled them to fight with one another.

From time to time I got sentenced to drive the kiddy carpool to school. And it was usually on a Monday morning. This added a new dimension to that dreaded time of the week.

It's not that there was anything specifically wrong with the kids, all about ten years old. In fact these Gen Xers were probably very normal. It must just have been the combined effects of this normalcy that pulled my strings.

The event started before I even left the house with Daniel. It usually unravelled something like this: Jason's mother, a woman a bit obsessive compulsive about being on time, phones to remind me to get to her house by 8:05, not a minute later. I erred once, having got stuck behind a school bus, and this lady wouldn't let me forget it. I remind her it's early. I envy the rooster. He's probably still fast asleep.

We leave at 7:55 and get to Richard's house. I beep my horn a couple of times and eventually Richard makes his sortie. I don't believe he hears my horn. Richard cannot possibly hear anything since he always has earphones glued to his ears, listening to loud music. I can clearly hear drums on steroids, blasting away. Likely so can my neighbour. And his neighbour. At this point I consider putting something into my cassette player to counteract his sounds, something more soothing, like "Hooked on Jackhammer Sounds."

The next stop is Adam's house. This kid is actually OK. It's just that for some reason his mother insists on loading him up with books, lunch, writing implements, sneakers, and other paraphernalia that she attempts to stuff into this large knapsack. She presumes that the carpool this morning is being driven by the gentlemen of Allied Van Lines. I try to persuade her at the top of my lungs that there is absolutely no room for this stuff. Only Richard, The Earless, is oblivious to the discussion.

I exit the car, and after some effort Adam's mother and I manage to stuff his freight into the trunk. We open the trunk again quickly as Mom notices a six pack of Del Monte fruit cups on the driveway. I have no doubt that this gear contains enough provisions to sustain Ottawa. And I'm glad that we aren't travelling over the 401 highway this morning. Otherwise I would be obligated to pull over at a scale stop.

We then hit Jason's house, at 8:07. His mother is out there on the drive waving her index finger at me and giving me an earful. "Do you know what time it is? And Jason better not arrive late." At least I think that's what she's saying as I motion to Richard lend me his earphones. He refuses. I smile at Jason's mom and say, "No problem, Lady Macbeth." There's no way she can hear me.

Finally we pick up Shirley, our back-seat driver. This kid presumes that I have no concept of how to get to my son's Toronto school. She figures I live in North Bay. I just drove down 250 kilometres this morning for the pleasure of doing this carpool.

Shirley is indispensable. She not only insists that I "go left, go right, cut through the shopping plaza near the Royal Bank," she also tells me when I'm going too fast.

Jason jumps in and says I'm going too slow "like a snail, we'll be late," he whines. (This I guess is the other side of the coin on Shakespeare's schoolboy.) The two of them argue over the sweet strains of Richard's vignettes of thunder.

By succumbing to Shirley's navigational directions, I end up on a side street behind this great big school bus. The bus, stop lights flashing, naturally is in the process of embarking about three hundred kids.

Jason, fearing we'll be late, slaps his head. I hold onto my head, fearing what his mother will want to do with it. My only hope is to open my trunk and go through Adam's gear. Chances are he probably has a makeshift helicopter inside. Or maybe even a makeshift school. With teachers. We can camp here for the day. Maybe there's even an embassy in there. I'll seek asylum.

The school bus leaves. We continue our trek.

Suddenly a squabble breaks out in the car. Jason says, "Adam's lunch stinks." This is followed by, "Adam just pinched me." As I slow down and look into the rear-view mirror, I suddenly take on a role secondary to a transporter. I now feel like a wrestling referee as Jason and Adam poke one another, I'm tempted to ask them to stop while I announce them properly: "In the back-centre seat, wearing blue shorts and holding an ET lunchbox is Jason. His opponent, in the back driver's side, wearing blue jeans and a Star Wars T-shirt, is Adam. This morning's referee is dad Marcel. Jason and Adam please shake hands."

We boomer parents became de facto mediators and arbitrators. We became the forerunners of today's alternative-resolution culture.

With Shirley's further navigational aid and the accompaniment of The Who, or whoever's strains I hear coming from Richard's sound system, we cruise into the school lot as the bell rings. At least I think I hear bells.

The kids pile out as if the car's on fire. Adam says, "What about my 'knapsack'?" I look around but I don't see a forklift I can borrow. Using my limited knowledge of Archimedes' principles, I pry the crate out of the trunk. My knowledge is quite limited, as my aching back tells me.

Oh, only to have a normal Monday morning! As an aside, Adam's lunch did have a pungent odor. I was certain he was holding a large Cheddar hostage.

And these kids were today's Generation Xers. Little do they recall.

Disciplinary Dinosaurs

What three words best describe Gen-X kids? Simple: Spoiled, spoiled, and spoiled. Totally. Baby boomers' parents did not love their kids any less, but they expressed their love differently. For example, I speak of corporal punishment. These parents experienced a world war, and they knew life was full of hard knocks. And generally they didn't hesitate to remind their kids about some of these knocks.

If you misbehaved, on a good day they would give you a warning or send you to your room or deny you a privilege such a television. Our parents for the most part were not our friends or equals. They were the boss. And their job description endorsed the maxim "Spare the rod and spoil the child." My own parents, I will say, did not go in too much for the rod part of it. And if they did have any ideas about that rod, I was a quick runner and able to make a getaway until the situation cooled down. However, occasionally I would find myself running into my father's hand and after that collision, I found that standing for a bit was my most comfortable position.

Many parents, however, were more into the rod part of it. More specifically it was the father's belt. In addition to holding up his pants, the strap served an alternative purpose as a weapon of mass destruction. Or should I say "ass destruction."

I can almost see a salesman in a clothing store trying to sell a belt to a customer and describing its qualities. "This belt is genuine leather. It should hold up your pants for years. And it slips off easily if you want to spoil your kid."

I recall an incident in juvenile court one day. My client had shoplifted a small item and the judge let my Gen-X kid client, parents at his side, off with a warning saying, "Jared, I'm happy to see you acknowledge that stealing a set of headphones from Best Buy was wrong. I know I won't be seeing you again in my court. You have a good son there, Mr. and Mrs. Cooper."

During the recess, the court registrar, being about my vintage, who raised his eyebrows during the hearing, said, "Had I done that as a kid, the juvenile court would have been at the end of my father's shoe."

In other words, the parents generally sided with the authorities. This included the school. If you got nailed for misbehaving in school, you generally did not benefit from the maxim, "What happens in school, stays in school." It didn't stay in school.

If word got out you committed a felony, such as mimicking your teacher while her back was turned, or pulling a girl's pigtails, or accidentally spilling an ink well (some of us remember those), and this matter resulted in your getting sent to the principal, whatever he did to you, your parents might add a bonus. The parents of baby boomers, especially the earlier ones, were not your best choice for a court of appeal. As I said earlier, traditionalist parents in those days were not overly aware of or concerned about the legal principle of double jeopardy.

In my school days, the dreaded school punishment was the strap. Actually, in my school it was not a leather strap. It looked more like a foot-long flat wooden spatula. One would think the principal bought it at IKEA. Flip your burgers on Sunday, clean it off, and it's ready for use on Monday to rap a few knuckles.

You'd get sent to the principal's office and be told by his secretary, usually with a name like "Miss Wallace," to have a seat outside. Actually, I think all principal's secretaries were called Miss Wallace. I digress, again.

Generally there'd be a couple of other felon students seated just outside the principal's office waiting for school justice to be served. You might call the area "Strap row."

The secretary seemed to enjoy seeing the kids squirm. She would smile and in a low voice, cackle. She obviously got a high being part of this reign of terror. In fact, she actually bore a close resemblance to Charles Dickens' *Tale of Two Cities'* Madame Defarge. I was tempted to get her an appropriate Christmas gift, like a set of knitting needles. It wouldn't surprise me at all that if you Google the name "Wallace" you'll get "do you mean Defarge?"

Actually, I had the pleasure only once. My heart rate certainly rose as I entered the principal's chamber. It did not help when Mr. Webster denied my request for a blindfold. He didn't even offer me a cigarette. Then again, smoking a cigarette on school grounds was the reason I was sent to him to start with. I'd say he was a bit hypocritical. Before he did his thing, he carefully placed his own smoke into his ashtray. The event was somewhat traumatic. I wonder whether I can still sue IKEA.

Corporal punishment was also imposed for other victimless crimes. I heard several stories from Catholic women who noted that they were lefties and if their nun teachers noticed them writing with their left hand, they would give them a whack with a ruler. Being a lefty myself, I found these stories spooky. I suppose the nuns thought there was something sinister about being a southpaw. I asked one of these survivor lefty ladies what they gathered from this experience and she said, philosophically, "I hate nuns."

I wonder if there were ever any left-handed popes. I Googled "left-handed popes" and all I gathered was that as about 10% of the population is left-handed, likely 10% of the popes were southpaws. But no names came up, there being a suggestion that those who were may have had it banged out of them as schoolchildren. I guess those nuns, or perhaps monks, had no idea they were whacking the hand of some poor kid called Antonio whoever, who one day will be called something like Innocent VII. If it were me, I'd revisit the school and track down that monk and say, "Ah huh! Friar, you're excommunicated!"

As I scanned Google, I did see names of famous lefties such as Bill Gates, Aristotle, and Leonardo da Vinci. But these weren't popes. Sorry. I imagine the church would never divulge a left-handed pope scandal.

Once again, I digress.

Generation Xers of course were all spared corporal punishment, for the most part. If my son were ever sent to the principal's office, he wouldn't ask for a cigarette. He'd insist on making a call to his lawyer.

Even belts have undergone a cataclysmic change. They're not all leather anymore. I see ads all over on Amazon and elsewhere advertising "vegan" belts. I guess the children of parents who buy one would be safe from corporal punishment. After all, which parent will go out of their way to buy a vegan belt and use it to tan their kid's tuchis? Then again, I certainly wouldn't want to get struck with a belt made out of zucchini.

And with my kids, we never endorsed corporal punishment. We had a fair but firm warning system. If one of my kids stepped out of line, we'd give him or her a fair warning. "Danny, please move your Monopoly game off the kitchen table."

After a few minutes of his ignoring this request, and still staring down on a milk bottle token sitting on B & O Railroad, I'd say something like, "I still see the Monopoly set on the table. Remove it now or else."

The "or else" definitely was effective. It would make his wheels spin, wondering what happens if he leaves the game there. That element of doubt, or uncertainty, about the potential sanction for disobedience got him thinking. He'd respond obediently saying, "In a minute dad."

We always taught our kids to be reasonable. I suppose that response was reasonable. I guess he was not overly concerned about my sending him directly to jail.

After another couple of minutes, the game is still on the kitchen table. I give him an ultimatum as I stare impatiently at a hotel on Marvin Gardens, and I'd say, "I'm counting down from ten."

He listens and acts. "Be there soon dad." As my countdown progresses from ten to one, I slow down, "three ... two ... one ... one-half ...

Nothing doing. There was no way I was going less than one-half. That's my final price. I start losing my patience. I say, "OK, this is it. One-half, one-quarter, zero." I lower my price; parents must be flexible.

This is it. I remove the tokens from the Monopoly game. Daniel jumps up saying, "Dad, what are you doing? You just removed your own hotel from Boardwalk. I landed there and haven't paid you rent yet. This means I land there free."

Looks like I cut off my nose to spite the face. Being a parent isn't easy.

He then helps me tidy up the game, declaring himself the winner. I accepted the fact that parents must make sacrifices for their kids. Boomers were softer on discipline than their parents were.

What would my dad have done in the situation? He would give us a first and only warning, like a weather watch. He'd say, "I'm hungry, remove that game from the table now."

If the game were still there after a minute or so, he'd descend upon it and swoop it up like Dorothy's tornado and toss it into his room. I'm sure the event would cause the shares of Shortline and B & O Railroads to plummet. I sense that this would not be a good time to tell him I just passed GO and to ask him for the $200.

Actually, the situation is totally hypothetical. I never owned a Monopoly game as a kid. My parents never splurged the $6 or so to buy me one. You want something, earn it. I'd have to find the money. I never did. I was hoping for a bank error in my favour, but that never happened.

Generation Xers were spoiled generally in more ways than one. Boomers felt compelled to give their kids amenities and benefits their parents could generally not afford, or thought not essential, like music lessons.

My (Brief) Music Career

As a kid I wanted to play the violin. (Which kid didn't?) After some nudging, my father succumbed and we visited a nearby music school in my Montreal working-class neighbourhood. I got the feeling the place was not exactly the Julliard School. It was called something like "Bert's Music Academy." The logo was a treble clef. I never said Bert was imaginative.

My dad and I attended and met with Bert. We both took the meeting seriously. I wanted to enroll, and my dad wanted the best deal, meaning economy and some assurance from Bert that I would come out of the institute after about four weeks with skills and proficiency rivalling Itzhak Perlman. I don't recall the entire conversation, but at one point my father did mention the "Place des Arts." This venue, Montreal's equivalent of Carnegie Hall, exceeded my expectations, at least for now. I never said my dad didn't have a sense of humour.

There was a big hitch in the discussion at one point. After my father and Bert worked out a deal for the lessons, so many dollars per month, Bert asked him if I had my own violin. Naturally, this took my dad by surprise. How and why would I have my own violin? I didn't even own a harmonica. Or a Monopoly game.

Bert told us that we would have to rent a violin from him, at an additional cost of $5 per month. This totally unexpected cost rattled my father. He turned to me and said in Yiddish, "goniff," meaning "thief."

I nodded my head in agreement. After all, five bucks was serious money for a simple violin rental. It was not as if we were renting a Stradivarius.

He and Bert each lit up a cigarette and they went into a heavy negotiation session. My music career hung in the balance. I thought it best not to interrupt and ask for a smoke as well.

I recall Bert showing my dad different violins, and even some other musical instruments, presumably cheaper to rent. My dad noticed a cello nearby, which Bert said rented for $6 per month. He told Bert that the violin I wanted to play should go for much less as it was much smaller than that big one. Bert gave my dad a curious look.

I was concerned the two would come up with some more economical-to-rent instrument, thereby ending my violin career. The only cheaper item I could think of was a conductor's baton. Now which kid on earth wants to learn how to play that? It doesn't even make a sound! And who wants to brag about being a conductor? I watched *Fantasia* twice and there was no way I wanted anyone to look at me and say, "There goes Leopold Stokowski."

After a few more minutes and cigarette puffs, the two came to a deal. I was now enrolled as a pupil of Bert's Music Academy. I walked out of the place proudly carrying an old violin in a beat-up case. To me it was a Stradivarius indeed. My career as a virtuoso violinist started. Place des Arts, here I come. This was just the first step. Unfortunately, little did I know, there were not going to be too many more steps.

I was learning to play a string instrument, but alas, my family was on a shoestring budget. Unless I was going to show rapid progress, my days as the next Itzhak Perlman were numbered.

The first lesson consisted of Bert teaching me some basic notes. This was followed by a few violin strokes, which unfortunately were not too melodic. While practising diligently at home, I had an audience of one. My dad. Judging by his look, presumably he expected Beethoven's Violin Concerto. What I managed to muster was something sounding like an emergency amber alert broadcasted if a child goes missing.

Over the next lesson or two, my musical talents did not impress my father. When he watched me after about lesson three, he didn't even pause to light up a cigarette. Within the month, my father decided to shut it down and we returned the violin to Bert. I recall there was still one lesson owing to me for the month. Bert asked if I wanted it. This was my final music lesson ever. I recall the tune to this day. Any member of the public upon hearing it would consider going out and looking for that missing child.

I certainly felt sad about having to stifle my music career. I felt a bit desperate. At that point I almost felt like asking what it would cost to take baton lessons.

I will say that I somewhat revisited my music career as an adult. I eventually bought myself a small harmonica.

Incidentally, I don't know whatever became of Bert.

Natalie's Music Career (Also Brief)

The situation was different with the Generation Xers, the boomers' kids. I am talking 180-degree different. Not only were our children going to fulfill their musical aspirations, they were also going to take music lessons—because it was good for them. After all, we came from a place where we got our aspirations snuffed out for economic or cultural reasons, but we were not going to repeat the mistakes our traditionalist parents made with their children. We decided to make our own mistakes.

My wife and I decided our kids were going to get all the music lessons they wanted. The operative word was wanted. We asked our daughter, Natalie, whether she would like to learn to play the piano. We didn't even think about the potential cost of renting one. Knowing she'd practise diligently, we went out and bought one.

We found a piano teacher who was popular in the area. We attended at her academy, that is, her home. She named her price and we said fine. Like I said, we did not repeat the mistakes of our parents. We made our own. She asked whether we had a piano and we proudly answered, "Of course, Svetlana." What kind of parents did she think we were?

She made no promises, adding only one caveat—that our daughter would have to practise in between lessons. Sounded reasonable to us. After all, how could it be otherwise; Natalie did ask us for piano lessons.

The lessons started, and soon into them she mastered her first tune, "Twinkle, Twinkle, Little Star." We did expect a bit more, but to us it sounded like a Mozart composition. Actually, "Twinkle" is said to have been a favourite of Wolfgang Amadeus himself.

After a short while, Natalie began asking if she could defer a practice. Given the progress she was making, we saw no harm in her running her own plan. I certainly was not going to hover over her like my dad did over my violin practices. We did hear some faint sounds coming from the family room where the piano was that sounded like the quarterly chimes of Big Ben. We thought that was part of the lesson's regime.

Svetlana did ask us a couple of times whether our daughter was practising diligently. We said she was, though we were cutting her some slack. After a few weeks, Svetlana arranged the first music recital for her pupils. Natalie told us we would like it.

The grand inaugural recital was held in a room at a local community centre. There were about a dozen or so kids under the age of ten accompanied by their proud parents and many grandparents.

Natalie was actually the leadoff performer. She sat down on the piano stool and with the confidence and poise of Liberace, banged out two minutes of "Twinkle, Twinkle."

It was not what we fully expected. I was a little disappointed in that I felt the kid could have learned more after a few weeks of lessons. At least she stopped after that last twinkle and did not do a grand finale Big Ben.

I didn't bother telling my father about the event as I well knew his sentiments. And there was only so much fatherly laughter I was in the mood for. He probably would have asked me what it cost to rent that piano.

We thought maybe we should be a bit more assertive, for the kid's own good. I said, "Natalie, you cannot watch *Sesame Street* now. You have to practise your piano lessons." She responded with understanding, "That's no fair. It's child abuse."

As my wife and I persisted, Natalie shouted back her allegations, each time a few decibels louder. I rushed over to close the window to prevent a charge on my house by any good Samaritans who might be standing outside wondering where the cries for help were coming from.

I thought of her choice of words, "child abuse," and wondered, what if she's right? Relaxing on my recliner, I drift into a bit of a daydream.

Natalie's homeroom schoolteacher observes her and decides to have her checked out by the school psychologist—nothing unusual except that the child spends the entire morning doodling treble clefs.

Unbeknownst to my wife and me, a special musical abuse team at the local Children's Aid studies Natalie's actions carefully, looking for telltale signs such as toe tapping. In response to increasing incidents of musical abuse, the team has been set up jointly by the Ministries of Health and Cultural Affairs. The handpicked team consists of a doctor, a social worker, and a musicologist.

"Look at her tender fingertips," says the doctor. "I'd say these tips are consistent with the child hitting piano keys three to four hours a day." They decide to run some tests. The musicologist gets Natalie to say, "La-la-la" ten times, hoping he can pick up a trace of a Beethoven sonata. To the untrained ear, the "la-la-la's" would be indistinguishable from regular "la-la-la's," but the musicologist, Prof. Illich Zydelshtein, is the best in his field. The other day, the doctor asked him to check out some calluses on the feet of a six-year-old girl. It didn't take him five minutes to conclude beyond reasonable doubt that the kid had been forced to spend two hours a day in front of a mirror practising *Swan Lake*.

It seems this month has been a heavy one for Tchaikovsky. Just last week, the professor diagnosed a seven-year-old boy as having suffered an overdose of the 1812 Overture. On a hunch, when police were sent to the child's house to question the parents, they recovered two French horns, a trumpet, and a cannon.

The team completes my daughter's assessment and concludes that indeed there has been musical abuse. The social worker swings into action and summons the police special unit, "Nutcracker," to my house.

The cops descend on my home, led by ragged Lieutenant Luciano Poletti, a baritone. Without further ado, they arrest my wife and me, and as evidence they seize our metronome. They also bring along for the raid, Mendelssohn, a beagle specially trained to sniff out hidden musical instruments. The dog must be having an off day as he walks right by our living-room piano.

The police briefly question and then also remove our other two children, including my teenage son, Daniel, who says he'll tell them everything they want to know. He leads them upstairs to his room, where they locate a clarinet—under a Monopoly game. Lieutenant Poletti puts the clarinet into a plastic bag. The lieutenant also comes across an arsenal of reeds, enough to keep a kid playing clarinet for five years.

My wife and I are charged with musical abuse of our children. Pending trial, the kids are sent to a foster home where they're guaranteed a music-free environment, the foster parents playing only Rolling Stones tapes.

At our trial, the prosecution claims that parents have no right to impose musical training on children. Reams of classical lesson notebooks are introduced as evidence. The prosecution even introduces a toy rubber cello discovered by Mendelssohn.

My wife decides to exaggerate a bit and tells the court that it was all an accident. The testimony given by Prof. Zydelshtein in response, however, is powerful and damning. He says that my daughter's "la-la-la's" are no accident: "These are la-la-la's in C major. No accident. No way."

We ultimately get convicted and the prosecutor goes for our jugulars, and our vocal cords. He demands a sentence to the penitentiary.

Our lawyer demands more money. We've already given her the money we'd set aside for the children's music lessons.

We don't want to go to jail. Prison justice for this type of offence is swift. I recently read about a father doing time for musical abuse who was attacked by an inmate with a trombone that he'd carved out of soap.

"No! No!" I cry out. I snap out of my daydream. The house is peaceful except for an awful screeching sound apparently emanating from Daniel's clarinet. I run upstairs to his room, yank his clarinet away, and say, "No way. This could be dangerous. Play Monopoly instead."

More Spoilage

Boomers felt the need to spoil our kids, giving them everything our parents never or rarely gave us. These benefits ranged from fancier vacations to enhanced birthday parties to driving privileges.

As for the latter, my father never let me drive his car. I never argued with him about it. In fact, we never owned a car. I am certain his reason for foregoing this acquisition was his fear of driving, or rather his mistrust of other drivers. Whenever the news reported a serious accident where a bus collided with a car, he would say, "See, a bus is safer." In retrospect, I regret not pushing it; maybe I should have asked him to buy a bus.

I bought my first car at age twenty-seven, a few days before number one son, Daniel, was born and before I got called to the Bar. I don't believe in astrology, but maybe given it all happened in the same month, just maybe this lineup of the stars and constellations made Daniel, as he was growing up, relentlessly bug me to allow him to drive the car. True, I do read the horoscopes sometimes and I never once saw a reading like, "March 11th. Pisces, your lucky day. Ask your dad to let you drive the car."

The kid used to love to sit in my lap at a parking lot and keep his hands on the steering wheel. It was the best I could offer him at age four. My own dad never shared this joy with me. How I wish he would have been a bus driver.

As for vacations, a summer vacation for my parents meant sharing a house with a couple of families in the Laurentian Mountains an hour or so north of Montreal. For about two months, the kids would have breakfast, run out and play tag or chess (Monopoly?), or swim in the lake, return for lunch, repeat aforementioned activities, and so on.

An out-of-town trip for the most part meant you visited places where your hotel would be your uncle's house. And what if you wanted to visit a place that was devoid of a friendly relative? This happened only once we had our own kids, the Gen Xers. We took our first major trip to Cape Cod when our son Daniel was two. It was a real splurge and a plunge to spend about $25 per night at a local "near the beach motel." Albert Einstein would have said something like "distance, like time, is relative." After all, being on a cape, the beach couldn't have been that far, relatively speaking of course. But it was there, eventually.

And on the way back home to Montreal, it was getting dark and we decided to stop for the night in Burlington, Vermont. Accommodations were sparse, and the Holiday Inn had limited space available—for $33/night. I had already raised the bar to $25 in Cape Cod, and that to me seemed like spending it at the Ritz. I looked at Daniel and asked him if we should do a big splurge that night. We decided to go for it, taking his light snoring as a yes. After all, it was for the kid.

I Now Declare Your Birthday Party Open

Another sign of boomers being the transition generation from the traditional to the modern era was in how we celebrated events, like birthday parties. They were definitely more organized and less spontaneous.

This was evident in the foods, the decorations, and the amusement activities. Actually, it was also evident in the frequency of having a birthday party altogether. My parents threw a party for me at ages five and six. And that was it. Their view was that I've already had two parties in my formative years and that should hold me. I can now safely proceed to develop and grow up.

We have three great kids, one Xer and two millennials. I cannot remember a year during their pre-teen years where we dared miss making them a birthday party. I'm sure, had we missed one, some snoopy neighbour would have reported us to Children's Aid, resulting in an investigation by some social worker. Speaking of child abuse, her report would no doubt conclude that we were unfit parents and that our kids were children in need of protection. Doing birthday parties certainly kept us under the radar.

Then there were the activities themselves. In my childhood days, generally few. The kids would gather, sit where they wanted and start munching. They amused themselves spontaneously by some shoving and teasing. You'd hear the cacophony of chatter suddenly punctuated by, say, a girl saying, "Marky says my hair is short like a boy. He's calling me "Tillie Willie."

None of the parents freaked out, assessing the psychological damage taking place. Tillie's mom would say, "Call him Mark the Park." This would result in Mark complaining, "I hate Tillie. She called me a park."

In spite of these indelible experiences, we all grew up basically adjusted OK. No birthday party in my kiddie days was complete without the kids exchanging jokes like, "Why did the moron throw the butter out the window? Because he wanted to see the butterfly."

These jokes kept us in constant giggles. Just try telling jokes like that about morons today. The morons of the 1950s and early '60s have all vanished. There simply aren't any more morons. Where did they go? Maybe they all sailed around near the Bermuda Triangle. After all, they were morons. Who knows?

And the word itself would draw instant censure from the vigilant parents. For that matter, given the frenzy with plant-based foods, so would the word "butter."

Boomers did not want to repeat the mistakes their traditional parents made in raising us, so we decided that birthday parties need outside assistance to be fulfilling. After careful deliberation for our son Daniel's sixth birthday, we hired a clown. I recall his name was Bagel. Bagel the clown.

He was a bit late in arriving. As the kids were getting restless, I went out of the house in anticipation of spotting Bagel's arrival. I saw a couple of cars moving along the street slowly but his was not one of them. As I stood in front of my house anxiously awaiting the arrival of that clown, I thought of that scene in Alfred Hitchcock's *North by Northwest*, where Cary Grant is standing on some remote road in rural Iowa anxiously awaiting a crucial contact whom he expects to arrive by car, but who actually flies over in a crop duster and tries to eliminate him.

Finally I noticed a Chevy Nova cruising at a couple of kilometres per hour. The driver had a big red nose, a mop-style red hair wig, and his face was painted white. He appeared to be looking for a house. I went over to his car and as he rolled down the window, I said, "Bagel?" (It's the lawyer in me; always that element of doubt.)

He nodded and held out his hand for a high five. I emitted a sigh of relief. Could have been worse. He could have sprayed me with seltzer. Or even worse. I will say I did take a quick gander up at the sky for that crop duster.

The clown needed no introductions. It seems Bagel was a popular event at the time, performing at numerous birthday parties. As he entered, some of the kids shouted, "It's Bagel. Hi Bagel. Remember me?" Of course he did.

Bagel spent the next forty-five minutes or so doing silly magic tricks, leading the kids in some sing-song, and of course creating balloon animals. I am not sure whether these days at birthday parties clowns would create plant-based balloon structures. To date nobody ever told me he saw a clown who can turn a green balloon into an avocado.

Having paid guests or entertainers was not an option for most boomer kids' parties. When we were growing up, clowns did not belong at birthday parties. They belonged in the circus. Full stop. At least even suggesting a clown for my birthday party would have given my dad a hearty laugh.

Then there were the foods themselves. Sugar was king. There was always an assortment of candies, ice cream, and a huge birthday cake. The kids all left the event well preserved.

The parties we made for our kids were more gourmet. Of course we still had the cake and ice cream, but at least we also ordered out to ensure nutritional goals were satisfied. To meet these standards we ordered in pizza. After all, aside from being sodium loaded, it's not junk food per se. It was usually a party size, meaning it was square-shaped.

We generally had to accommodate some specific dietary requests. There was always a kid who did not want a corner piece. On one occasion one such kid when served this offensive pizza slice actually threw a tantrum, tossing this vile square across the table. My inclination was to ask Bagel the clown whether he could do some magic and turn the whole pizza into an inner-parts-only pizza, no outer corners. Actually, that was my second inclination. The first was whether he could make the kid disappear.

But there were some legitimate understandable dietary concerns as well. Allergies. The late 1970s and 1980s saw the proliferation of food allergies, many life threatening as the victim could go into anaphylactic shock.

I don't recall one instance of a kid having a food allergy in the 1950s or '60s. The prominent allergy then was to ragweed and feathers. This generally wouldn't affect how you cater birthday parties. The kids were usually safe. You never heard of a parent ordering a birthday cake loaded with chocolate chips, coloured sprinkles, and goose feathers.

The next generation for some inexplicable reason was plagued with serious food allergies, the prominent ones being peanuts, nuts, dairy products, eggs, or fish. Parents usually alerted the hosting parents of their kid's allergy and it was up to us to provide an alternative culinary serving. You generally received a subtle call from a parent saying something like, "Jason is allergic to dairy products; if he tastes any he can die." We got the point. This admonishment would mean you'd have to ensure you do not serve Jason pizza. Square or otherwise.

The standby for dairy anaphylactic kids was a tuna sandwich. Jason appreciated the concern, querying, "There's no pizza in here is there?" No problem.

Naturally, there was often some kid, like Jeremy, who was severely allergic to fish. You would serve this kid pizza no problem. You just had to be careful not to confuse Jeremy with Jason. Good thing nobody was allergic to just corner pizza.

Another popular allergy, very lethal, was peanuts. Our son Gabriel is a beneficiary of this allergy. He, like other kids carries an EpiPen, which can be a lifesaving shot of adrenalin in the event of accidentally ingesting the allergen. When he would go to a birthday party in the 1980s and '90s, we'd call ahead to make sure the featured *plat du jour* wasn't a peanut butter sandwich.

All of this was unheard of in the 1950s. Party food had no restrictions allergy-wise. The biggest calamity you might find at a birthday party was the squaring off between Tillie Willie and Mark the Park.

I don't know what changed starting in the Gen-X years; I suspect it's something environmental, like Chernobyl. And the Chernobyls and similar nuclear-reactor leaks and disasters they never told us about.

I once chatted with a gentleman who lived not far from Chernobyl when it busted. He said that within a couple of days of the leakage, which wasn't fully disclosed by the authorities, he saw some flies in his office that were the size of golf balls. He thought that was "unusual."

True, I am not a scientist and I can't speak with authority on the subject, but I just sense that there is a connection between these nuclear leaks and the allergies. I heard that a long time after that nuclear reactor in Fukushima, Japan, cracked, leaking stuff into the waters, some fish turned up across the Pacific on the shores of British Columbia—with two or three heads. I thought that was unusual. It would certainly make me think twice before serving that tuna sandwich to Jason. Or was it Jeremy?

And as I write, we have a new allergy. People. We have to social distance. Where is all of this heading? Wouldn't it be nice if Bagel the clown could make it all go away?

Guns, Chicken Fingers, Stethoscopes, and Other Dangerous Paraphernalia

Boomers and their kids were also characterized by the gifts they gave and received. Buying gifts for boomers was easy. The gifts of choice for girls were dolls and for boys, guns. And each gender appreciated these standard stereotypic-issue gifts.

To this day I recall getting a slew of guns for my sixth birthday. My arsenal was the envy of the street. One exception. I recall one of my guests did not get me a gun. He got me a toy doctor's set. It included a stethoscope, some popsicle sticks as tongue depressors, and a box of coloured candies representing pills.

I suppose you can say the doctor's kit complemented the gun collection. After you "shoot" your target, he may need medical attention, and what best to have handy? Your doctor's kit.

Given that I now was the neighbourhood doctor, as well as the gunslinger of course, I took my role as a medic seriously. On one occasion, too seriously. During some wild-west game we were playing, my neighbour Izzie Markovitz fell to the ground shouting he had been hit by an arrow. Given that this game did not involve any "Indians," we thought his claim of being wounded was frivolous. Nonetheless, it was not for the doctor to judge his patient. I went over to Izzie and though he supposedly suffered an arrow injury between the shoulder blades, after giving him a once over with my stethoscope, I asked him to open his mouth and say "ahhh" while I shoved a popsicle stick halfway down his gullet.

Unfortunately, we all got more than we bargained for as Izzie's gag reflex kicked in and out it all came. The game ended abruptly. Izzie's mother ran out and I recall she was not too appreciative of my efforts at first aid. She actually called me "crazy." That certainly was no way to speak to the doctor. Good thing she never sued me for malpractice.

Then again, it was Izzie's fault. My medical steps were standard and necessary. Every first-year medical student knows that if the patient complains about getting stuck by an arrow in his back, you must examine his throat. Badda bing badda boom.

I will say, however, that I did give my medical aspirations a rest for a long while. Then again, I can't say the practice of law always drew more appreciation from the public.

Getting back to those guns, they were usually cap guns. Most of the guys idolized the cowboy. Our heroes were gun-toting slingers like Roy Rogers, Wild Bill Hickock, Wyatt Earp, and the like. I even got a couple of black Lone Ranger masks as well. (Not recommended for COVID-19.)

Another hero was Davy Crockett, who unfortunately met his demise in 1836 at the Alamo. One of my guests brought me a Davy Crockett raccoon-fur hat. I guess this type of gift would not go over too well these days. PETA would probably tar and feather me. Excuse me, tar and plant-based feather me.

Another guest brought me the Davy Crockett rifle, "Old Betsy," to go with it. I swung it around like Davy did on the Alamo ramparts, clubbing Santa Anna's invading force. At least that's what Davy did according to the Disney version of history.

Guess what? This stash of rifles, six shooters, cork guns, and others did not make me or other contemporaries violent. Somehow we viewed these gifts as fun objects you played games with. I even got a Derringer, the type used by John Wilkes Booth. This gift did not create a propensity in me to want to sneak into a theatre and seek out an unsuspecting president.

Maybe they served as some type of release for our fantasies and that was it. A toy gun was just that, a toy gun and nothing more.

I actually brought one of my six shooters, in a holster, to my school for show and tell. The kids were impressed. Even the teacher admired it, opening a discussion about Wyatt Earp and the gunfight at O.K. Corral. That's when I first heard about one of the participants on the good side, "Doc" Holliday. This information validated my understanding of the need to have a doctor at gunfights.

Then again, I also found out later that Doc Holliday was not a physician; he was a dentist. Downer. Had Izzie Markovitz complained about getting struck by an arrow in the teeth, there would not have been too much use for my services. For that matter, as a kid I never once saw a toy "dentist set." I imagine it would be too costly to produce. You have any idea what the chair alone would go for?

That teacher, Mr. Halpern, and the class also discussed sheriffs and law and order. Maybe these types of discussions had an influence on my nurturing an admiration for the law and becoming a lawyer. Who knows?

Perish the thought of a similar scenario unfolding these days. Firstly, of course, you would not see guests dare bring toy weapons for their birthday kids. If they did, they'd never clear the metal detectors.

Even pretend-pretend weapons are governed by the zero-tolerance test. There was a kid in grade school in Alabama who in the lunchroom waved a chicken finger around shouting "bang bang." He was summarily suspended. Getting even more ridiculous, another kid I read about did not even bother with the chicken finger. In Columbus,

Ohio, a school suspended a ten-year-old for pointing his fingers like a gun. The school noted that the kid turned his fingers into a "level two lookalike firearm."

I guess to some schools, zero-tolerance violence means just that. Ignorance of the rules is no excuse. Any duffer by now should know that extending your forefinger and folding in your next three fingers turns your hand into a level two lookalike firearm. With a gesture like this one, the kid could easily hold up a level two lookalike bank.

I actually Googled level two firearms, and the Wikipedia list includes machine guns, sawed-off shotguns, and grenades. Let's face it. That Columbus school made a prudent call. Who's to say the kid wasn't going to pull off one of his fingers and toss his fist into the crowded class.

I guess it wasn't the fact that it was a finger or a chicken finger. The chicken was a red herring. We just live in crazy times.

Even right here in Toronto, one school doesn't allow the students to refer to the term "bullets" when describing the symbol used to make a list stand out from a body of text. The children must call them "cupcakes."

I sure hope none of these kids ever decide to become police officers. What will they carry on their belts should they need to defend themselves in a shootout? A spatula?

Unlike the boomer generation, our kids took their arsenal to another level, feasting not on classical weapons but rather on futuristic ones.

The 1970s saw the arrival of films and television series such as *Star Trek*, *Star Wars*, and the like. What boomers bought for their kids were entire spacecrafts, such as the *Starship Enterprise*, replete with advanced futuristic not-even-invented-yet weaponry. So if your child brought a replica of this flying armoury to school for show and tell, he would be received with open arms. We are talking about a spacecraft that could, with a press of a button, annihilate ten thousand Klingons. Or maybe more depending how magnanimous the kid felt that morning.

Nor would there have been a problem for Luke Skywalker to get and show off a Darth Vader lightsaber. He could bring a set of two to school and give a sound-and-light fencing demo at recess.

But heaven help the kid nowadays if he or she leaves the *Enterprise* at home and playfully just uses a finger with some sound effects. The culprit would be suspended for violating the zero-violence school-board policy. And naturally the story would go viral—another tool in the campaign against aggression. It is comforting to know that these schools play such an important role in preventing violence.

Good thing our lawmakers have not made it mandatory to obtain a licence to use our fingers. The reason this did not happen yet, at least in the USA, is that likely such restrictions would violate the Second Amendment. I'm sure it would receive stiff opposition from organizations like the American NRA. If the good Lord would have wanted us not to use our fingers as weapons, he would not have equipped our hands with a pointer.

Boomers are indeed the sandwich generation. We went from a world of innocence and common sense to a mad, mad, mad world. At least it's "progressive."

And this is also a good a time as any to discuss health.

CHAPTER FOUR

As Long as You're Healthy, Seventy Is the New Fifty, of Course!

The only way to keep your health is to eat what you don't want,
drink what you don't like, and do what you'd rather not.
~ Mark Twain

OK boomers, do we take good health for granted? That is the question. How often do we take stock of our health and express joy? I have yet to hear or see anybody say, "I can see," and then follow this up with a run up the steps of some iconic museum and do a Rocky victory dance. And as you get older, running up those stairs doesn't get any easier. There is some wear and tear with the mileage. This is as good a time as any to do a head-to-toe physical of aging.

Eye, Eye

At the ripe old age of six, I was prescribed eyeglasses. I would subsequently get my eyes checked about annually, spending a boring fifteen minutes reading random letters on a screen. The ophthalmologist, Dr. Shapiro, would say something medically sounding, like, "Uhmm hmmm." I sensed that he was equally bored. I was OK with that, scowling at my mother for dragging me here annually.

The years rolled on, like they always do and at age forty-five-ish, and my ophthalmologist, a different one by now, examined my eyes and uttered the further medical words, "Ahhh!" He asked if I had ever heard of bifocals. What came to mind was a picture of Benjamin Franklin, being the guy who invented bifocals. I suppose he did that while he wasn't flying his kite.

My eye doctor told me my eyes had changed with age. This was natural. He said I would now require multi-focals. This I guess was an improvement over those bifocals, which had that stupid horizontal line across the middle of the lens.

My first reaction was one of anger. I thought to myself that there is no way I resemble Benjamin Franklin, balding, with spectacles on his nose, sporting a weird grin; in short, a poster boy for an old fart. No way was I going to switch to multi-focals.

A week later my wife, Shoshana, and I were at Costco. While she checked out some sweaters, I sort of drifted to the optical counter. It was not far from the toiletries shelf and I needed some shampoo anyway. I asked the optician where the shampoo was. He was rather devious I'd say, as I ended up walking out with an order for a pair of multi-focal glasses. To be fair, he referred to them as "progressive lenses." I felt a bit better, as unlike bifocals, or even multi-focals, that phraseology did not trigger a picture of that old fart.

But it was a wakeup call that I was no longer a little boy with eyeglasses. Something was happening to my body. I wasn't crazy about it. At least, on the positive side, I left Costco with a giant tub of Head and Shoulders. And it was on sale.

Speaking of heads and shoulders, let's work our way down a bit, to the arm.

Blood Pressure, What, Me Worry?

Blood pressure. For years many visits to the doctor would include a blood pressure check. And for years I considered the process of a trained professional spending his or her time squeezing a small balloon, as if they were inflating a bicycle tire, while having a stethoscope in their ear—amusing. No doctor ever commented during those years. Not even a casual, "Uhm mm hmmm."

Then, one afternoon in my late forties, after an invigorating event where I argued with another lawyer, I attended at the office of my doctor, Dr. Katz, for some minor matter, and after his usual mandatory BP check, he uttered some other medical term, like "Uh oh!" This was the first time a physician had actually crossed that line of my perceived immortality and uttered an "uh oh."

I came of age into the world of hypertension. It was not long after that one thing led to another and I was soon introduced to medication. My first was referred to as a water pill. I did try alternative routes. These included relaxation exercises: Breathing differently, mediating, imagining peaceful settings, and so on. But life does not always accord you all the baubles and extravagances you want. Telling a litigation lawyer to relax is like telling Maple Leafs superstar Austen Mathews to dribble the puck on a breakaway, and as he approaches his opponent's net, not take a shot. When an opposing lawyer delivers a thick brief of documents for a court motion, requiring you to scramble and respond within hours, I found it did not help me much to envisage a gently running meandering brook in the Laurentian mountains. It's not as if I could just toss that brief into the brook.

I also looked into dietary changes. Reduce sodium. I went that route for a while and found no change in my BP readings after switching to low-salt Pringles. Eating fish was also recommended. Especially salmon. Sounded good to me. I even saw a YouTube by chance about bears in the wilds of British Columbia catching salmon as the fish swam upstream while spawning. That was encouraging. But it didn't alter my readings much. I don't know how eating all that salmon affects the bears' blood pressure. I just can't imagine a grizzly sitting down comfortably in Dr. Katz's office and allowing the good doctor to put that cuff around his paw and then squeeze that balloon. I can say seeing Yogi Bear sitting in the waiting room might just raise the BP of some of the other patients.

I will say, before accepting that water pill, I did ask my doctor whether I could just drink more water. He gave me a definitive medical answer: "Nope."

There's more. The good thing is with aging you are not limited to two strikes before being called out. The bad thing, however, is with aging you are not limited to two strikes. There's more that can go wrong. Let's head south.

The *P* Word, or Rather, the Pee Word: Prostate

The third strike arrived as I hit the late fifties. The medical term is "enlarged prostate." In English that's BPH. *B* does not stand for "big," but rather for "benign." Actually, there is little benign about it. Starting from the doctor's examination. I'm not a physician but I can safely say the orifice of interest in this exam is designed for one-way traffic. Out. You don't need a built-in road sign to demonstrate this point.

And this is one time you feel more reassured when you know for sure you have done nothing to annoy the doctor, or worse, the doctor's receptionist. You don't want to see her whisper anything to the physician as he puts on his glove before your examination.

At these times, I sometimes think about the father of medicine, Hippocrates. I wonder if and how he conducted a prostate examination. I'd guess he likely got the patient to affirm and agree not to whack him after the exam. This would add a new dimension to the Hippocratic Oath.

The buzzword for men's prostate issues is "PSA." This is the acronym for prostate-specific antigen. I suppose it's called PSA as many of us can't remember something like, prostate-specific antigen. (Actually, I'll deal with memory issues later; if I remember.)

PSA is determined by a simple blood test that should be done at least annually if you are over fifty. (By the way, being a retired lawyer, I shall hereby add a disclaimer that nothing I say should be taken as offering medical advice. Mind you, I don't mind if you want to address me as "Doctor." That would be nice.)

As the years roll on, in addition to talking sports, men start blabbing about their PSA scores. "Hey, Hank, the Leafs beat the Rangers 5 to 2 last night. Mathews got a hat trick. And I just got my PSAs back. 4.6.

"Mathews is hot, Chuck. As for your 4.6, I'll raise you two. I'm 4.8."

Size does matter.

And what exactly is a prostate all about? It is generally characterized as a gland about the size of a walnut. The problem is that as a guy ages, the walnut starts getting enlarged, whereby it presses on your bladder. You don't have to be Dr. Albert Schweitzer to figure out what that means.

Enlarged prostate symptoms are generally characterized by peeing characteristics such as frequency, urgency, or slowly. Frequency means just that. It's all about, here we go again. And again. And the plumbing system does not take a break during the night when you're asleep. I keep a flashlight and a baseball bat next to my bed. I need the flashlight to ensure I don't trip on my usual two or three treks to the washroom—and to ensure that I get there in the shortest distance. I keep the baseball bat near me in the event that my house gets invaded by burglars. No, I am not kinky at all.

Urgency means just that. When I travel on the highway, I can't rely on promises of a "rest area in 40 kilometres." My favourite sign is "McDonalds, next exit." And I assure you my purpose is not to get a Big Mac. I'm sure I speak for a large percentage of the getting-there male population.

And if I use a bus service, I usually check ahead and ask if there is a toilet on the bus. I don't want to be that obvious; I try to be discreet. I'll ask questions such as, "Is this bus an express?" I'll continue with something like amenities on the bus, such as Wi-Fi or USB port and what have you. Then I'll casually ask, "Is there a discount for seniors?" At that point I expect the agent to tell me, "And of course the bus is equipped with a toilet." If that doesn't happen, I'll say, "Never mind the express part of it. And I don't care about that stupid Wi-Fi or USB port. Does the bus have a can?"

My aim to be discreet has limits. I recall once travelling on a charter bus in England from a cruise terminal in Dover to London's Heathrow Airport. The trip was to take over two hours. I was told by the shore excursion desk on the boat that the bus was toilet equipped. On that assurance I had a fine breakfast, including an extra cup of coffee. When we boarded the bus, I noticed the bus, or "coach" as the British call it, had no toilet. Or rather, as the Brits would call it, no "loo." What does a man do with no loo?

I was a good boy for about an hour and a half until Mr. Walnut got into action. I knew I'd never make it to Heathrow. I had to make contingency plans for a safe landing. I had a good idea of what Captain Sullenberger felt like after some birds disabled his aircraft over New York and he had to land it in the Hudson River.

I walked over to the driver, a gentleman likely in his early thirties, and told him about the upcoming crisis. He told me that as we were on a major highway, we would have to wait until we got to the "services." Stopping at the side of the highway was not an option. (I did suggest just that.) This is one time I regretted travelling on a major thruway. I would have had no problem had we been going along a country road in a place like Sherwood Forest. I don't think Robin Hood would have disturbed me.

The promised services were about fifteen minutes away. That does not sound too bad unless your bladder feels like the size of the Hindenburg. For those fifteen minutes I was in desperation. Had I had a choice of the arrival of those "services" or the coming of the Messiah, I would have said to Messiah, "Can I get back to you soon?"

Fortunately, I made it, terra firma. Of interest is that once we stopped, about twenty other men on the bus rushed out and made a mad dash to the "services." A number of them thanked me for getting the driver to pull over. I don't know how they knew what I told him when I went up front to make my frantic plea. Then again, they looked at me and likely had a good idea. After all, they are men too.

As for the driver, I noticed he did not even visit the lavatory. In fact, he actually bought himself a cup of tea. Like I said, he was probably in his early thirties. A little pisher. We all knew what he'd be in for a few years down the road.

Another problem with an enlarged prostate is that voiding your bladder sometimes takes a little longer than expected. If you're ever lined up at a public washroom waiting for a urinal, you'd be wise to eyeball the relative ages of the guys in line. It is not generally a great idea to line up behind someone who looks like Moses. When they stand there endlessly, they are waiting for something and it isn't Godot.

And the bladder, given the pressures on it from the prostate, does not always void in the first stream. The process is nothing at all like Old Faithful. You often think you're done (as does the guy behind you, the young guy I should say), but you just know you are about to experience a sequel. And you do. It all doesn't necessarily end with strike three.

Hear, Hear

Unfortunately, aging also brings about changes to your audio system. Sometime into my sixties I noticed that I could not catch fully what people were saying. I found myself asking them to repeat some words, or to crank up the volume. I also noticed that while watching a movie on say, Netflix, when the screen offered language choice, I pressed "subtitles."

My kids readily picked up on this issue and suggested I go for a hearing test. I found myself going into denial. My answer was, "Why would I have hearing problems? I have never had any before."

In addition to not hearing some words at all, I often heard the wrong word. Seems the brain works overtime to make sure you get the best information your ears can relay. So if someone tells you there is a sale at a store nearby, what might get filtered to your brain is "there is a hailstorm coming by."

What really brought this to light for me was an experience I had on a cruise ship. It was the first dinner in the mammoth dining room. Shoshana and I were seated at a table for eight. At one point the waiter accompanied a younger couple and seated them at our table. There was lots of chatter in the hall. The rather attractive lady sitting next to me and I started talking, and while making introductions I had difficulty making out fully what she was saying. I did catch that she was from Utrecht in the Netherlands. When I asked her what her occupation was, she told me she was a prosecutor. But I did not hear "prosecutor," I heard "prostitute."

Hey, Amsterdam's red-light district needs no introduction. We all know the world's oldest profession readily thrives in Holland. The Dutch are famous for more than their windmills, tulips, and herring. I certainly was not surprised by her answer. I figured she was taking a well-deserved vacation. I also figured this was going to be a rather interesting cruise, given the occupation of my tablemate. Certainly at least as interesting as sitting next to another guest at my table, a tax accountant.

Her answer piqued my curiosity and prompted some further banter. I asked, "They also have them in Utrecht?'

She replied, "They have them in nineteen regions across Holland."

Interesting I thought. Business must be booming in the industry. I continued, "Are you self-employed?"

She seemed surprised at the question and responded, "Why no. I work for the government."

Now I have heard of health care being nationalized in some places in Europe, but this? I queried, "Why does the government need them?"

Even more puzzled than before, she answered, "To deal with the criminals of course."

I thought to myself, the Netherlands' justice system is certainly enlightening. Was this provision of penal benevolence found in the Hague Convention? In Canada, where I live, judges usually sentence criminals to time in the slammer, or to pay fines, or at least to do community services. I was indeed curious about what crime a guy has to commit to warrant intervention of a lady of the evening.

It was not until another minute or two of conversation that it hit me that my ears had played yet another trick on me. I guessed my brain hadn't caught "prosecutor," and it offered me what it thought was a reasonable alternative facsimile. And I had run with it.

I did tell my wife, Shoshana, about this incident. After a hearty laugh, we concluded that after we got home I would go for a hearing test. They do have audiologists in Toronto—and other regions no doubt.

A hearing test is another rite of passage in life's journey. This is much different than getting eyeglasses. Little kids can get eyeglasses and that's OK. When I was a kid some nasty other kids called me "four eyes." But many famous people wore glasses and it's nothing to be ashamed of. I've already mentioned Benjamin Franklin. You know that old fart. Moving fast forward, the list includes Elton John, Johnny Depp, and John Lennon. Glasses can be cool.

The situation, in most cases, is different for hearing aids. What comes to mind are those massive foot-long horns you see in cartoon images, held against his ear by some sap who resembles Methuselah, who asks the person addressing him to shout into the end of the horn. I'd rather be called four eyes than Ferdinand the bull. Any day.

When I think of famous deaf people, who comes to mind first is Beethoven. (At least he did not have to wear glasses.) Interestingly, Vienna has a "Beethoven house." I should say fourteen Beethoven houses. The reason for so many of them is that his co-tenants and neighbours would complain about the noise Ludwig was creating, and so his landlords kept on evicting him. Imagine that!

When you ask for a hearing test, you are saying to yourself, "What gives? I must be getting old. Maybe I should compose a symphony."

I was a bit uneasy in going through the procedure. I had to pick a hearing clinic where I could be assured some privacy and dignity, and feel comfortable. Once again, I decided to do it at a local Costco. I had my reasons. If I met anyone I did not want to divulge my issue to, I could tell him, "They have a super sale this week on eggplants."

I approached the hearing centre gingerly and with trepidation. The audiologist ushered me into a little room the size of a tiny igloo. Within that room was a small isolation booth. It resembled those isolation booths you'd see on those Miss America pageants (or former pageants?), where a finalist contestant gets cloistered so she cannot hear some crucial question being asked of another contestant outside the box. I put on earphones and we were all set. I commented to the audiologist, "And if I had one wish, I'd wish for peace on earth." I don't think she heard me.

The test consisted of identifying beeping sounds as they got fainter. If I thought I heard a beep, I had to press a handheld button that resembled those devices you see a World War II bombing crew press. Bombs away. If you either press when you shouldn't or fail to press when you should, you lose points. You can't ask the audiologist whether she heard that inaudible sound or not. I think that's ridiculous.

How are you supposed to press the button if you can't hear anything? Even a police-force trained bloodhound would be baffled.

The second part consists of the audiologist saying words in a low voice, which words you're supposed to repeat back to her. She would whisper words like "heart" or "meat" or "frog." I don't know how any mortal with normal hearing is supposed to accurately make out this gibberish. She did not say the word "prosecutor." Too bad, as I knew the answer to that one.

Not surprisingly I failed the test, with flying colours. The recommendation was hearing aids. I get the feeling this is the recommendation for everyone who undergoes this drill. It's like the one solution the veterinarians have when a horse has the misfortune of breaking a leg. Shoot!

I was not impressed with the diagnosis and resolved to pass on her recommendation. I did, however, leave Costco with three perfectly ripened eggplants.

As the months rolled by, I noticed that my hearing edge was a bit off. I would be asking people to repeat words. My daughter would say something like "boat," and I'd hear "moat." Hey, the brain can play tricks on you. And this interpretation wasn't totally unreasonable. Nothing unusual about a boat on the moat.

As some more months rolled by, my family convinced me to visit Costco again for a reprise. They actually first suggested that there was a sale on winter tires. I took the bait. One thing led to another and there I was, sitting in that booth again like Miss Alabama.

Same song. After the test, I was told my hearing had deteriorated somewhat since test one. I darted out, resolved that hearing aids may have been OK for Beethoven. But I didn't need them nor was I going to get them.

About two weeks later when I opened the kit, my kids helped me set up the hearing aid's Bluetooth. Welcome to the world of hearing loss. And given that Ludwig van Beethoven and I now have something in common, maybe I'll sit down soon and compose that symphony.

But it doesn't end there.

Strike Five: Cognitive

When I was younger, I could remember anything,
whether it happened or not.
~ Mark Twain

Cognitive issues can be a major matter as we move forward in years. These range from learning new skills to mood changes to memory. Why don't I start with memory (before I forget)?

I found as I was getting older that I forgot people's names. A matter would come up in my law practice and I would ask my able assistant for a file where there was a similar problem so I could see how I handled it then. Sometimes I could not recall the name. I was sure it began with the letter *R*. After telling Angela it's likely the Richardson or Rochon or Rosenberg file, she'd say, "Close. It's Henderson." Ahh. I thought so all along.

At times, on a good day, the answer would be close. For example, I was sure it reminded me of a precious metal. Silverberg? Silverman? Silver? The winning name would be Goldstein. At least that was closer than Henderson.

And of course it could get embarrassing when you look puzzled when you're face to face with the person, especially if he or she knows your name. He'll greet me saying, "Hi Marcel," and I don't know his name at all. The best I can respond is, "Yeah, it is a nice day today."

At times you get really close, and in these cases I take a shot at his name. Mustering a wave of confidence, I'll say, "Hi Mike." His response will be, "It's Mitch." The best retort I can then come up with is, "I know that. I'm just testing you."

Akin to forgetting a name, sometimes you know the guy's name, but he is the wrong guy. In your mind the gentleman with the bushy moustache is Gerald but he is actually Morton. We've confused him. At least we don't call him Stalin.

I find certain name-vanishing incidents repeat themselves. For example, I often forget the name of that musical *Mamma Mia!* I know most of the songs, but the title often plays hide-and-seek with me. I have tried to remember it by saying to myself that it reminds me of my mother. That's fine and good until I forget it again and then I don't remember whom it's supposed to remind me of. I don't even remember the "Mia."

At other times I have trouble recalling two similar words that mean the same thing. For example, I am talking about that statuette of a little man resembling Happy, one of Snow White's dwarfs. He is a gnome or a troll. Generally I remember one of these words at a time, but not at the same time. It takes me a while, and with luck, while I am good with "gnome," I remind myself to remember the first two letters have a silent combo, in that it is pronounced "nome." That generally works wonders until the issue comes up again and I see that cute little statue decorating some neighbourhood garden. I'll say, "That's a nice troll. What's that other word again?"

My wife will give me the hint, "You don't pronounce the first letter." That doesn't help much. I say "phone?" "knight?" "pneumonia?"

She says "wrong."

Of course, "wrong," the silent *W*. OK, "wrap?" "wrinkle?" Forget it, I'm good with "troll." It gets frustrating.

Another form of memory interruption is when you aren't sure why you are there. You enter the kitchen with a noble purpose in mind. But after you get there you aren't quite sure what that purpose was. Did I want to grab something to eat, put something away, check if the stove was off? The good thing is that after my frustrating retreat from the kitchen, it does hit me sooner or later. I remembered to go to the wall board and pick up the grocery list, which I created not to forget what to buy. Hey, we all need that shopping list.

Another memory problem is misplacing stuff. We are talking keys, clothing, pens, and so on. The good news, at least in my case, is that I have had that problem for ages. The bad news is, it doesn't get better with age. It gets worse as twenty-five years ago or so many of us didn't have cellphones. Now we have those smartphones to misplace. If they'd really be smart, they'd tell you where they're hiding.

At least you can telephone your mobile number and hope the ring is within earshot. And if you happen to have left it under the sofa cushion, you can probably shift the blame to the dog. Why not?

I recently took misplacing to a new dimension. I was visiting someone at Baycrest, a local institution consisting of a nursing home, geriatric hospital, and social recreational centre for the elderly. I saw a bulletin board with a notice about a free memory assessment. It piqued my interest (though I don't recall having a significant problem recollecting stuff). The exercise would be for academic purposes only. The notice had a telephone number to call and the number was noted on little tear strips. I ripped off a strip.

Again, though I don't really have a significant memory problem at all, after a couple of days I thought I would give them a call.

Unfortunately, I couldn't locate the phone number strip. I had misplaced it. Oh well, like I said, the exercise would have been for academic purposes only.

And what do we call memory disruption? There are a number of expressions associated with this annoyance. Some of them suggest you have no clue about exactly what you are trying to remember. You "draw a blank." It doesn't get much worse than that.

You might say, "For the life of me, I don't recall." This one demonstrates improper grammar. That is another problem. Maybe it went "in one ear and out the other." We've already discussed hearing issues. I definitely remember doing so. Then there are the expressions that suggest there is some hope or expectation in recalling—whatever it is. In that case, "It's at the tip of my tongue." That at least is better than drawing a blank. Who wants a blank on the tip of their tongue? There's hope. Similarly, it may not be at the tip of your tongue but "it rings a bell." Maybe if that bell is loud enough, you'll remember what you aren't remembering. Then again, to hear it you may just need those hearing aids. And we've gone through that, haven't we?

Then there are those expressions that to me display arrogance. The speaker sounds as though he or she remembers, but do they? They'll say something like, "My car is making this noise. We probably have to replace that "whatchamacallit." If that doesn't fix the noise, maybe the problem is the "doohickey"? And if all fails, it will not surprise me if the culprit is that "thingy."

Of course when you don't recall what exactly it is, why not go more generic and still maintain your air of knowledge. The problem definitely is under the hood, "yadda, yadda, yadda." I'd really entrust my car to this person.

And speaking of knowledge, back a couple of decades ago when we baby boomers were in college, the caricature of memory issues was the "absent-minded professor." There may be some substance to this one. I read once that Albert Einstein boarded a streetcar in some German city and the conductor asked him where to? The prof suddenly forgot, hesitated, and got off the streetcar. It happens to the best of us. Maybe he was having what we now call a "senior's moment."

The question then is, what can we do to lessen these forgetful episodes? You want to be able to remember quicker or to "jog your memory." Sometimes to help you, as you are about to make a comment, the person you are addressing will tell you to "hold that thought." The problem with that is you have it there and then. It's even beyond the tip of your tongue. By holding onto it, you risk it's escaping. Then when you try to find it, you draw that inevitable blank. Or you might try writing it down. That generally works as long as you remember where you wrote it down. For that matter you may not remember again to even look for the note. Alas!

A stereotype for remembering to do something is tying a string around your finger. That might work, sometimes, especially if you remember what that string was all about. And generally it's not a reminder to buy dental floss.

What you don't need are reminders from the likes of creditors, even though they are just "friendly reminders."

And how do we try to remember names, especially if they are at the tip of our tongues? If you really have "no clue," you run the alphabet. At least you know the gender. I'll do a few A's, like Allan, Albert, and Andrew and work my way along. As I get past M or so, I start getting nervous. I am still hopeful it will "hit me." If it doesn't hit me after Peter, Paul, or Perry, I get frantic. I always skip over the letter Q. After all, who names their kid something like "Quid"? I try to remain optimistic. I may even jump ahead a bit and try "Zach."

If it does not "come to me," I try sleeping on it. I find that often works. Within hours or a couple of days, when I least expect it, it will "just surface," like a submarine. I'll be, say, on the subway and suddenly I utter audibly, "Casper!" Last time I did that, a millennial got up and gave me her seat.

Sometimes you just know it begins with the letter *M*. After shouting out Mary, Marilyn, Marlene, Maureen, and Marisa, I get a bit frustrated. I then ask my wife for a hint. What is the second letter of the name? She'll tell me it won't help. I insist she toe the line with me and help me end this agony. She'll say her name is Francis. Ugh. At least it's not Queenie.

I once ran memory issues by a geriatric physician who, when I practised law, used to do medical legal assessments for my injured elderly clients. She told me that not recalling names and such right away was likely as a result of data overwhelm. Too much on your mind at one time. If you remember that you cannot remember, your mind is still OK. This was worth remembering. It made me happy. Which brings us to another emotion, happiness.

If You're Happy and You Know It Clap Your Hands

Don't cry because it's over, smile because it happened.
~ Dr. Seuss

Although we can be moody at any age, aging per se can bring with it more potential for discouragement, depression, anxiety, or whatever you want to label it.

Actually, I don't have to label it at all. I am not a shrink. And that is a good thing. I doubt a shrink can make you feel much better talking about aging than I can. A psychiatrist certainly won't do a better job making you lighten up a little more.

A shrink will do two things. Listen to your lamentations and say, "Uh-huh. I see." Then the shrink or shrinkette will prescribe pills to try to lift your spirits. They don't even have those couches you see in the movies. That alone would cause me distress. Bummer.

Let's psychoanalyze the moods of older people. We fall into three categories: sort-of-happy, more likely less-happy-than-we'd-like-to-be, and undecided-for-sure.

I sometimes envy the sort-of-happy guys. Maybe. They'll appear cheerful, they'll tell you they live life to the fullest, and they'll indulge in weird activities, like playing pickleball. It all does make sense to a certain extent. But are they happy?

The less-happy-than-we'd-like-to-be also makes sense. After all, we are now in the sunset years of our lives. What of it? I have had the pleasure of watching sunsets now and then over an ocean or a lake, and those are indeed memorable moments. But for some reason, hitting the sixties and beyond doesn't evoke this bliss.

For one, our friends start dropping like flies. Our newspaper reading habits shift a bit, and instead of the sports or the financial pages, we develop an inexplicable interest to first see who died. Your mind goes from, "That's the news, now for the weather" to "Never mind the news? Who died?" More about this issue later.

And I have already discussed health matters. With age, things rarely improve. It's like expecting gravity to think it over and reverse.

You can change parts in your computer or get a new muffler for your car. But you can't really replace body parts. Oh yes, I know when your hip or knee goes, you can get a replacement. But this too comes with pain, long waits, and rehab issues. It's quite a lot to have to endure just to be able to play pickleball.

Maybe some of the sting in this mood is mitigated and softened in that you stop getting those pesky calls from life insurance agents.

Then we have the undecided-for-sure group. I like this group the most. They talk little if asked about aging. They generally respond with sounds and gestures. When asked how things are, they grunt, "Agh!" or "Neh" or "Umm." I'm OK with that. It beats hearing, "I live my life to the fullest."

Or they'll gesture, shrugging their shoulders, waving their hand in a dismissive motion, or give you a thumbs up. The latter doesn't mean things are good. More likely their thumb is stuck; they are suffering from arthritis.

Can happiness be achieved in your golden years? Sure. This is a good a time to go over some theories of happiness. What is happiness?

The gurus believe they have the answers. They conduct studies, asking brilliant questions such as: "Are you happy? (a) most of the time, (b) some of the time, or (c) leave me alone, you should only have my problems." They conclude something like Calcutta's inhabitants are 14% happier than Budapest's.

Here are the common threads I've noticed. Read on if you are less happy than you'd like to be. If you are happy you obviously already know the answers.

Money? Uh-huh. Money brings a temporary high. They talk of lottery winners who felt great initially but actually were soon gloomy as they could not adjust to their new wealth. I suppose if you had a chat with a lottery winner you would hear him say, "Ah, those days before winning the fifteen million dollars in SuperLotto—we had a huge mortgage, the finance company owned the Camry, and we could not afford Charlie's braces—those were the good old days."

So if it's not money, then love? Love makes the world go around. King Solomon had one thousand wives. Was he happy? Who knows? He went around saying, "Everything is vanity." I'm not so sure. With one thousand wives at least you no longer have to waste time with online dating services.

Is happiness having the right job? Like a professional athlete? Athletes have both fame and fortune. Alas, how often you see them in misery. We see baseball players sitting in their dugouts, utterly dejected as their team is down 9-0 in the eighth inning. Pay me ten million dollars US a year and I'll find a way to smile at the camera. Many of us would be thrilled just to get a good seat to watch the game. And here is a guy who gets to see the game for free from ground level, and he's not happy. What gives?

What about professionals? Certainly not the happiest. My dentist always reminds me that dentists have one of the highest suicide rates. I suppose the rate spikes for dentists living in Budapest.

And being a lawyer, I can certainly confirm that many of my colleague legal beagles do not explode with ecstasy after the judge in the case they spent three years preparing for says, "I don't believe a word your client says. I'm surprised you ever took on this frivolous file. Case is dismissed."

Could the answer be religion? The crusaders certainly thought so. Thousands came from Europe, dressed in smart tunics bearing embroidered red crosses, to the Holy Land expecting to make the infidels happier by imposing Christianity. It didn't make anyone happier, except maybe the tailors.

The problem with religion is that there are no guarantees to getting what you pray for. You hear people say, "If I win that lottery, I'll be good. I'll give half of it to charity." And what happens if they don't win? They question the existence of a higher being and feel miserable. This is when love can kick in. Your partner can utter those comforting words, "Money isn't everything." You get philosophical and you feel happier, right? Wrong. You'll likely say, "Why did that unemployed janitor from Quebec win the fifteen million dollars? I deserve it more."

Which brings us to the philosophical angle: attitude. Be positive. The glass is half full, not half empty. I actually did this experiment. I filled up a glass of water 50%. I then muttered, "This glass is half full." You know what? It did not make me feel any better.

The gurus also preach gratitude. Be grateful for good health. I find that works, for a while. I took my temperature and it was 36.5 Celsius. I said to myself, "Hey, my temperature is normal." That experiment really lifted my spirits.

I decided to maintain the momentum. I filled that glass to the brim and said, "Hey, now the glass is 100% full." That didn't exactly make me a paragon of ecstasy.

The studies then drop the big downer. What if the propensity for happiness is mostly genetic? Maybe those guys in Calcutta have more happy genes than the residents of Budapest. In that case, are we stuck at the level of happiness we are preprogrammed to have? Get me a drink.

As we can see, the quest for happiness can elude all generations, not only us boomers. It may therefore be best not to be overly crabby at some of the foibles of aging and follow the advice of the good Dr. Seuss and try to smile at the good that happened.

And speaking of the good that happened, we come to technology. Then again, is it all good that happened? Let's have a look.

CHAPTER FIVE

The Curses (and OK, Maybe the Blessings) of Technology

Respect older people. They graduated school
without Google or Wikipedia.
~ Author unknown

L ooks like even Google doesn't know the author of that one.

What generally stresses baby boomers and seniors the most these days? Other than pandemics, I'd say the top three are failing health; finances; and rapidly changing, unintelligible, and in-your-face technology. Personally, I also hate it when I'm in an Italian restaurant and people near me ask the server to douse their pasta with Parmesan cheese. The vile odour is devastating. But that is another matter.

Let me deal with technology now as, unlike health or finances, where there is a doctor or financial advisor or banker to speak to, in the tech world we are often cast into an impersonal milieu, having to deal with machines, robots, and such. As well, you may get the idea from the epigraph that begins this chapter that technology bothers me a bit.

I suppose some people will also stress about the environment or climate change, or whatever you want to call weather taking its natural course as it has a been for zillions of years. I'll just call it "weather taking its natural course for zillions of years." I don't think about it one way or the other. If it's cold in Toronto, I put on my Canada Goose coat and I feel great. I don't know what it's lined with but if it happens to be goose feathers, those geese who contributed did not do so in vain. Anyway, most Canada geese do not suffer the scourges of a Canadian winter as they head south in the late fall. They're not stupid. That's why folks like us are called snowbirds. Probably those birds who hesitate too much get caught and end up being part of a winter coat.

When summer comes, bringing with it scorching temperatures, I open my air conditioning. Anybody have a problem with that? If you do, show me how my getting some well-deserved comfort will cause some icebergs to melt in the next twenty years, resulting in the relocation of polar bears.

If anyone does have a problem with what I do, let me know and I'll send you a manual fan. I'll promise to make sure it's not made of feathers. Can I use paper products? Likely not. Can't cut down trees. What about cloth? Don't know. Is it made in a fair-trade "sustainable" way? Who knows? Sorry, I tried. You'll just have to cool off by blowing on one another.

Then again, I'm not sure millennials will know about this non-tech manual solution for cooling off. For temperature control we now have the Nest. This outfit, owned by Google, will install a thermostat-type device in your house, allowing you to control your temperature even by remote, via your cellphone. It also comes with optional security cameras, which is not a bad thing. If I get a message that there is a break-in at my home, I can activate the sound and ask the thief if he's comfortable. If not, I can adjust the temperature by remote. If he tells me he's cold, I can always display some benevolence and direct him to my Canada Goose coat. Which all brings me back to technology.

I Am Not a Luddite

I'll start by saying that I am not a Luddite. Luddites were a group of English bands in the early 1800s who went around smashing machinery in work places such as cotton and woollen mills as they found this new technology threatening to their jobs.

The term today is often applied to technophobes. Again, I am not a Luddite. I never once stormed an Apple store. I'll save my pitchfork for the right moment. But I am mindful and fearful of the tech world.

Aside from how too many of the younger generation are obsessed with their smart devices, the world with the proliferation of technology has become too impersonal, made performing many simple transactions daunting tasks, and brought with it risks and dangers, including killing all privacy. Now that I have reinforced my feelings of depression on this subject, I'll try to maintain a sense of humour.

The other side of the coin is no good either. Some more history: The Commissioner of the United States Patent Office from 1898 to 1901, Charles Holland Duell, allegedly said in 1901, "Everything that can be invented has been invented." I'd say he certainly saw life through rose-coloured glasses.

If I were a budding inventor working on a major project, I'd hate to have to deal with this guy. This was only two years before the Wright brothers made their landmark airplane ride at Kitty Hawk, NC. I can just imagine the Wrights trying to get their invention patented while this visionary was in charge. They'd probably seek a personal meeting.

Wilbur W.: Sir, I see you rejected our patent application for the flying machine.

Duell: Ahem. It's already been invented. Those other brothers, the Montgolfiers, have a patent for the hot-air balloon. In fact, they successfully sent up a goat, a dog, and a chicken. What more can your "invention" supposedly achieve?

Orville W.: Well we have a machine that can one day fly people.

Duell: Pish tush! If people were meant to fly, the good lord would have equipped them with wings. Raise your arms. Let me have a look.

I wouldn't trust this guy to read my palm. He was no Nostradamus.

Charles Holland Duell went on to be appointed an appeals court judge in the Washington DC area. But in all fairness, there is commentary and suggestion that he never made this comment at all. Commentators point the finger at other people going back in history, people who certainly are no longer around or have nobody to defend against this accusation. They aren't sure.

Maybe it was Queen Victoria. After all, she was an important personality reigning for sixty-eight years until her death in 1901. She probably looked at a commode and said, "This is the greatest invention ever. Nothing else can possible top this. I am amused."

Or maybe the skeptic was Joseph-Ignace Guillotin, the inventor of the guillotine. During the French Revolution's Reign of Terror, he took a time out, and proud of his invention, perhaps said something like, "We have the guillotine, gunpowder, and wigs. Close the Bureau des Patents.

Unfortunately, Joseph-Ignace G. himself experienced the utilization of his own invention. When his executioner led him up the platform and asked him if he had any last words to say, Joseph Ignace could rightly have said, "Hey, mais oui! This thing has my name on it."

I suppose you can always attribute the Duell saying to Shakespeare. Actually, you can attribute any saying to Shakespeare. I haven't checked, but does he say anywhere, "A horse! A horse! My kingdom for a horse. I do doubt the future will ever create a faster mode of transportation."

Like I said, the other side of the coin isn't much better. Who would want to stay with the state of tech knowledge of 1901? No airplanes, no antibiotics, no stickie notes!

As for medicine, research shows that if a soldier during the Civil War suffered a bullet wound to, say, his leg, the doctor would remove it (the bullet that is). Unfortunately, he used the same unsterilized instruments on the previous soldier and there was no medication to prevent bacteria from spreading. This resulted in the wound getting infected and gangrenous, requiring amputation of the limb.

I suppose Charles Holland Duell was aware of this problem. I'd hate to think some hard-working scientist came up with an antiseptic solution or antibiotic drug back then and the patent office rejected it. "Hey, are you some type of charlatan peddling snake oil? We have all we need to deal with this medical matter. The surgical saw is the next best thing to sliced bread."

Maybe I am getting a bit ahead of myself, as sliced bread was not invented for another twenty years or so. But no thanks to Charles Holland Duell.

Nor would we want to otherwise remain in the horse-and-buggy age, unless maybe you're a closet blacksmith.

We are all happy with the comforts and conveniences, and inventions technology brings. Our problem is the baggage they also bring. Impersonality, complications and frustrations in performing transactions, loss of privacy, and other dangers.

Impersonality: It's Nothing Personal

We boomers grew up in an age where people dealt with people. Full stop. You wanted a hat, you went to a clothing store, a salesclerk would greet you, and you'd have a serious discussion—about anything. I'd mention the recent blizzard in Montreal, and he'd say, "Yep, there's more snow on its way." This would be followed by a French swear word or two. No problem. He wouldn't add, "All the fault of climate change."

He would then show me some hats. He'd give me his professional opinion as to why the grey one with the green feather was all me. I'd have to make an executive decision between it and the brown one without the feather. I'd decide the brown one without the feather was really me, take out the cash, and off I went. I had a new hat.

I can't say my choice was influenced by concern over the winged feather contributor. Again, hopefully some of his kin made it down south.

Today much of the commerce is online. The buzzwords are "visit us online." I doubt my kids in their thirties and forties, let alone my grandchildren, will soon know what a store is anymore. They'll ask, "Why would I go into that room and tell a stranger what I want to buy? That's private. Right?"

And I can't imagine wanting to buy that hat on Amazon and trying to have the same discussion I had with that salesclerk in that store in Montreal.

Customer (to Amazon): One brown hat, no feather please.

Amazon (Robot): OK. And did you know we're expecting a blizzard soon. Check out our sale on snow blowers.

Even at many supermarkets today, including Costco and Walmart, customers are urged to go to self-checkout machines. I avoid them, using them sparingly.

I enjoy human contact and I make it a point to joke around with the cashiers. As he or she charges up the salmon and potatoes, I might say something like, "I understand you have a special this week. Buy two pounds of potatoes and the salmon is free."

This usually elicits a smile or giggle from the otherwise bored cashier. Sometimes they joke back. One cashier replied, "Sir, that was last week's special." Another said, "Are we on *Candid Camera*?"

My comments always touch their senses of humour. The cashiers get uplifted as do the people in line near us who usually join in on the banter. One lady once added, "Let me go back for a moment and get more potatoes. "I have yet to have a cashier say, "No sir, the fish is not free." I have created a positive ripple of camaraderie in the world. Not necessarily big—just positive.

You cannot have this type of experience with a self-checkout machine at Walmart. If I'd scan the potatoes and the fish and then tell the machine about the free salmon special, if it were voice activated I doubt it would have a sense of humour. It would probably summon security: "Fish poacher at terminal three." At least the security guy would be a live person.

And very often, even if you try to access sites online where you wish to consider making a purchase, you have to run a gauntlet. You have to prove you're not a robot. The ironic thing is the system itself likely uses a robot to deal with us. Yet it will not deal with you unless you satisfy Hal that you are not one of him.

This is generally done in one of two annoying ways. The first is that checkerboard sketch that comes up showing say, street scenes.

You are asked to tick off all images showing something like a bus, or part thereof. This is not always as easy as it sounds as they often throw in something that could pass for a piece of a bus, like the back end of a San Francisco trolley. Get it wrong and you're back to square one. I just know the robot is laughing at me. I can't hear it but it's obvious.

Equally, or perhaps more annoying, is that test where you have to enter a code that they show you. It's never readily legible. It consists of several letters and numbers squished closely together so they overlap. A character or two is generally smudgy chubby, looking like it was created with a thumb dipped in an inkwell. (I won't explain what an inkwell is. First you have to know what ink is! Tough luck, younger generations.) Other times the characters appear in a weird font, like Middle Phoenician.

I am sure the robots are programmed by a millennial who read and enjoyed the Marquis de Sade's *The Power of Sadistic Thinking*.

But store experiences have also changed in many ways. Boomer, ever been to an Apple store? Apple actually is not just a computer system; it's a culture. For my birthday, my kids got me an Apple iPad. Initially I experienced little hitches and glitches, like how to operate it. I found myself having to attend an Apple store to get some support. That was an experience.

You go to an Apple store and what you see are swarms of clerks, or "team members," sporting navy-blue or red Apple sweatshirts. They are each distinguishable from one another by the tattoos they sport. That's not exactly accurate. You can also tell them apart by their body piercings.

As expected, all the staff are 110% tech savvy or perhaps tech saturated. You enter a store, and you get greeted by some millennial, usually with a name like Cal. You tell him you want to ask a question as you have just spent two hours trying to figure out why the delete button does not delete. Cal refers you to a colleague, usually with a name like Todd. Every Apple store has a Todd. Most, not all, also have a Cal.

Cal then sends a quick text to Todd describing your issue. Todd by the way is standing about one metre away from Cal. I suppose doing a ninety-degree turn and talking to Todd is not an option.

They also seem to know everything about you. When I recently attended and gave Cal my name, he said, "Hey, Marcel! I hope you enjoyed your scrambled eggs and whole-wheat toast this morning." He was pulling my leg. Or was he? He likely got this accurate information after clicking a couple of times on his Apple watch.

You do get the feeling that the staff treats you differently if you look as though you are over fifty-five years old. I have salt-and-pepper hair. (OK, mostly salt. OK, no pepper.) The guy at the front of the mall store, this time by the name of Zach, greeted me as though I were an Amish. The look he gave me clearly said, "I trust you found ample parking for thine horse and buggy."

I tried to hide my scratch pad and pencil, but it was too late. He asked me, "What are those strange implements thou art holding?"

As for the issues I had, my ten-year-old granddaughter, Laya, instantly confirmed the "delete" solution, showing me that on Apples you put the curser after, not before, the word. After her demo I certainly had an "Aha" moment. This makes eminent sense to me. I have no clue why Windows is so primitive.

I'm starting to get good at this. If anyone wishes more information on whether or not they should toss their PCs and switch to Apples, feel free to get in touch with me. Just give me a phone call. I implore you, however, please do not send me a text.

But perhaps the biggest lunacy is what's happening to our banks. They have no money; they're just a bank. Can we still bank on a bank? I don't know anymore.

I recently found a $100 banknote in my desk. I don't recall where it came from. But it made me happy—until I tried to use it at a supermarket. The cashier told me they do not accept $100 bills due to potential forgery issues. She virtually scolded me, stopping short of saying, "Nice try."

No problem. I visited my closest bank to get some smaller bills to avoid cashiers in the future looking at me as if I were fraud artist Bernie Madoff. The nearest bank was a CIBC. Actually, it could have been Scotiabank. They all look alike, at least from the outside.

I recalled that branch had been closed for a few weeks for renovations. There had been a sign posted on the door that read something like, "We are renovating in order to serve you better." I doubted that serving customers better was truly the reason for those renos. But I accepted those words as a reasonable excuse to temporarily deny me service.

As the branch was now open for business, I wandered in with my rogue $100 bill. Fortunately, there was no queue in front of the tellers. I soon realized why. The reason for this unexpected pleasure was that there were no tellers. I looked around incredulously and stepped outside for a second or two to look at the sign and make sure I was at a bank. Yep. No doubt it was a bank. There was that ubiquitous ATM, a huge ad with a colourful image touting the bank's generous interest rates for savings, and posters of piggy banks.

I went back in expecting to break that big bill. Then again, I suppose the Ottawa Senators expect to win the Stanley Cup this decade. As I stood bewildered, a young gentleman approached me, introducing himself as Tyler. Tyler inquisitively asked how I was today. After responding that I was fine, he asked if he could help me. I explained that I had just a short matter to transact and he directed me to an iPad on the counter. A bit puzzled about the innards of this bank, I made a comment about the necessity of being directed to an iPad and he assured me this place was indeed a bank and not an Apple store. He asked me to key in my name and noted that someone would assist me shortly.

A short half-hour later, another young person arrived, no doubt to continue to serve me better. She introduced herself as Amber. She asked how I was today. Still optimistic I could accomplish my mission regarding that $100 banknote, I assured her my emotional status had not changed since speaking to Tyler. I was still holding my own.

She asked how she could help me. I took out my $100 bill and asked if she could break it into tens and twenties. Amber gave me a surprised look, as if she had never seen money before. She said, "Sorry sir, but this is cashless bank." She looked at me as if I were Rip Van Winkle waking up after a twenty-year snooze.

I insisted she must be joking. She reiterated this was a cashless bank. I did not believe my ears. This was like Starbucks saying this is a coffeeless branch. Cappuccinos are a thing of the past. Give the barista your name and wait at the end of the counter, where in one minute you will get nothing. You're welcome to just come in and have fun taking up space and playing with your MacBook Pro.

Out of curiosity, I asked why it was cashless and she told me the banks want to help prevent money laundering. I was starting to lose my composure. First, I am rejected as being a potential forger and now I was facing disdain for money laundering. I insisted this note was all clean to start with. I told her I found the now-shunned banknote in my desk, not slipped to me on the sly by a shady character. I was adamant that my intentions were purely to get change for this pariah $100 so I could satisfy people, such as that suspicious supermarket cashier.

Amber did not budge. I even suggested I open a new savings account, using that $100 note as my opening deposit. I said I was interested in getting that high interest. I pointed to the image of that piggy bank. No go.

Before leaving the "bank," I asked her what would happen if a bank robber would come in and demand cash. She told me she would deal with him the same way. I did not ask her whether that included asking Jesse James to sign in on that iPad. There was little doubt in my mind she would. And that would be after introducing herself and asking how he was that day.

Then, as I was about to exit what, in my mind, used to be a bank, Amber added insult to injury by asking me, no doubt sincerely, "Is there anything else I can help you with today?"

Badda bing, badda boom.

I wondered about those bank renovations. The branch closed down for a few weeks and spent oodles of money so that when they reopened, they would not need to accept any money.

Meanwhile, here I am, still at square one. I need a small favour. Anyone have change for a C-note?

Your Call Is Important to Us!

It is not only dealing with a computer that brings frustration. Let's not forget voicemail. A little more history if you please. After all, your call is important to us—really, really.

Voicemail was unknown to boomers growing up. You called someone and if they were not home, the phone just rang a few times and we accepted that the recipient was unavailable. We did not generate a missing person report.

At one point, professional offices such as doctors' started subscribing to an answering service. This was useful as at least there was an actual person you could spill your guts to. I recall a number of times speaking to an answering-service lady whom I first thought was the doctor's nurse. I would tell her my kid is running a temperature. She would tell me she would pass the message over to the doctor, but meanwhile she gratuitously added that I give him some baby aspirin. At least there was some genuine concern.

Then came the answering machine. You leave a message after the beep. I suppose this was more economical than having nurse Jane take a message. The good thing was there was only one source to deal with. We all had dial phones (I shall not bother describing what these were as I doubt anyone under age fifty-five will be reading these words). You had no options. Just leave a message. You could of course leave a message there and then describe briefly what was wrong with your kid.

Finally, we jumped to voicemail jail. Suddenly your call was "important to us." You generally then had to navigate through options. No more live lady to explain the crisis to, nor even a machine where one message fits all. Your kid was sick and there was now no option to hit something like, "Press 7 if you think your kid is croaking."

Doctors' voicemails do first say, "If this is an emergency, please call 911 or go to the nearest hospital." Though sensible, I would expect something more creative. What else are you expected to do if you think you are going into cardiac arrest? Order a pizza?

Sometimes you get this robot at non-medical outfits that say something like, "My name is Emily. I can understand full sentences. Tell me what the problem is."

I doubt she does understand. I once wanted to test her and pull her leg and I responded, "My kid is running a temperature of 40 degrees Celsius and I believe that's a bit unusual." Emily came up with, "I believe you said it's 40 degrees Celsius outside. That is hot. If this is correct, say 'yes,' and please remember to stay on the line to answer a short survey about my service."

Like I said, we boomers experienced it all. From the old black dial phone to the Apple watch. I can't say which series. I won't ask Todd. Anyway there will likely be a new updated one tomorrow.

Boy oh boy, was Charles Holland Duell ever mistaken.

Complications and Frustrations—Enjoy!

Even if you decide to play the game and try to deal online, you are generally guaranteed to mess it up and get frustrated. And you deserve what you get.

My wife made the mistake once while we were in Florida of ordering a jacket online from some outfit. Doing it online meant she would save all of $10. OK, $10 US. That's about 13.5 Canadian loonies.

After spending fifteen minutes on her device, she glowingly said to me, "That was easy." She showed me the confirmation noting the jacket would arrive by UPS in three business days. We would get an email on the status of the delivery in a couple of days. Looked good to me. Too good actually.

I immediately noticed in the address that she had neglected to add our condo unit number, being one of dozens. No problem, we said. Let's go back and open the order and add the unit number.

Unfortunately, there was no way of doing that. The website only got you back to the beginning. We looked carefully and saw no tab reading, "Click here if you screwed up your address."

There were other tabs but not much more useful. We clicked on "About" and that raved about the company's products. It did say something like, "Our jackets are the finest. We'll deliver them right to your door, as long as we know where your door is." OK, I'm throwing in that last part. Bottom line, they didn't know where our door was. And that's what we were trying frantically to tell them.

We considered placing in a new order for a much cheaper item, this time with the full address, hoping there would be room for some comment from us like, "Hey, remember us? Please also send that jacket we just ordered to the same place." That too was not an option.

Then we noticed a "Contact us" button. There was actually a way of contacting them by telephone. We called the 800 number and we hit a voicemail robot called Isabel, who asked how she could help. There were numerous options, including billing, promotions, and more sales info. I got impatient at Isabel and told her that while I appreciated her efforts, I wanted to speak to a live person. Being an optimist, I did throw in, "Address error." She responded, "Your dress does not fit?" I tried.

Eventually I got through to someone, a Reuben, who spoke with a thick accent. I asked where he was and he replied, "Offshore." That sounded reassuring. I imagined some guy floating around in a raft off the coast of the Cayman Islands with a cellphone in hand trying to figure out a way to get rescued.

I told Reuben the problem and asked him to add the unit number. He said he can do that but that there was no guarantee this number would appear on my file for three business days. He asked how else he could help me. I told him that was all. I was tempted to ask if I could help him by maybe alerting the Cayman Islands Coast Guard. Who knows?

Before I was able to disconnect, a voice asked me to stay on the line to complete a survey. There was one rather broad question: "Was your problem resolved?" I shouted back, No. And go rescue Reuben." A voice answered. Thank you for participating in the survey."

Three days later, we received an email notifying us that the item we purchased had just left the UPS office in Pittsburgh and would be arriving at the UPS office in Charlotte, North Carolina, later that day. Given that we were in Naples, Florida, we had no clue why the jacket was making a pilgrimage firstly to Charlotte, North Carolina.

The email info had our address on it, sans the unit number. Reuben was right about not being able to guarantee the amendment to the order about the door.

The next day we received another email saying the package has arrived at a US Postal Service depot in Naples. Apparently it was going to make its final trek to our condo via the mailman. In order to save the poor mailman from trying to guess where we lived, we called the post office to see if we could pick the package up. Unfortunately, or rather very unfortunately, we could not get through. The message said, "Due to the high volume of calls we are experiencing, delays may be longer than usual. Expected waiting time is between eighty-eight and ninety-four-and-a-half minutes." In all fairness to the USPS, the voice did make a useful suggestion, noting that we could visit them online. Silly of me to ignore this sage advice.

We decided to grab the bull by the horns and visit the head Naples post office. We were a bit flustered to say the least. We were going to go postal, on the postal.

Ten minutes after arriving, we were somewhat successful. We figured out which line to stand in. Then it happened. While standing in a mid-sized queue, I noticed a gentleman walking by who looked like a senior employee and who looked like he was my vintage, greyish beard, glasses, and hearing aids. His name tag read "John." Unlike a Cal, a Todd, or a Zach, a John speaks to me.

I jumped in front of him and asked for some mercy and understanding, ending my one sentence pitch with the words "… online purchase hell."

He smiled and kindly said, "Of course, sir, come with me." John took some info from us at his desk and told us the package was there. *But* he could not give it to us as it was destined by the system to be delivered by the mailman. However, he took our unit number, added it to the info, and told us the mailman for the area, Bob, would deliver it the next day, between 11:15 and 11:55 a.m. A Bob also speaks to me. I looked at John like he was a saviour, Elijah the Prophet. Me not saying a word. He added, "Guaranteed." That's the stuff boomers are all about.

The next morning around 11:30 a.m., Bob delivered our package right to our door.

I thought about the ordeal that had lasted almost a week. In the end, my wife saved $10, and we went through a maze of bureaucracy dealing with impersonal personals. At least we had a gratifying and refreshing experience interacting with an old-school gentleman, going postal.

I don't know whatever happened to Reuben.

Privacy and Security—Ha, Ha, Ha!

Our next major problem with technology is erosion of privacy and hacking risks. Very often we have the choice to stay hidden, but we gratuitously toss it aside. I am talking about how we agree left and right to those terms and conditions.

I called my home insurance company recently to discuss a minor matter—like if I had coverage for a flood. Before I could proceed to speak to a live agent, the voice said something like, "To proceed with this call, we want to remind you that we can share all information about you with all parties we deem necessary in order to provide you with better service (of course). By proceeding with this call, you confirm that you understand and agree to our privacy terms and conditions. To find out more, you can visit our website and click on 'Privacy terms and conditions. Estimated read time, four hours and thirty-four minutes.'" It wasn't quite this forthcoming, but the ordeal was obvious.

I did take a quick look, and all I can say is that this read makes Tolstoy's *War and Peace* look like a pamphlet. I am a lawyer and I never read them. Nor can I think of any mortal with time on his hands who would, outside of a guy in a penitentiary.

You get this everywhere.

I happened to be at a Starbucks once and I decided to access their free Wi-Fi. Not surprisingly, you have to click on and accept their terms and conditions. I opened the link and I believe I am probably the only person who ever read this stuff, other than maybe the lawyer who drafted it after graduating from Attila the Hun Law School. Draconian? You decide. They go something like this:

Privacy?

- Ha, ha, ha! We have the right to share all your user information with necessary third parties. Necessary third parties include Starbucks, Google, and Amazon. As well, your personal information may find itself on Mark Zuckerberg's Facebook page. If you see it there, you hereby agree to like it.

- We have the right to install cookies of our choice on your device. Today we are installing blueberry scones.

Improper Use of Wi-Fi

- You agree not to use your device for any improper purposes including spam, copyright infringement, or defamatory postings. If you burn yourself on the hot coffee or tea, you agree to limit your reactions to saying "ouch."

- You may not transmit viruses, worms, or Trojan horses. You will be required to clean up any mess made by any such horses.

Offensive Language

- You will not use offensive terms, phrases, or language, including Canadian. These include but are not limited to the words "Timbits," "double-double," or "zed."

Damages

- You use this service at your own risk. We are not responsible for damages, injuries, or traumas, however caused, other than those governed by the 2013 Sumatran Java Convention. In such case, damages will be limited to one venti cappuccino (275 calories). For strawberry or vanilla extract please add fifty cents.

As the old adage says, "There is no such thing as a free latte." Is there anybody who doesn't click "agree"?

And do you sometimes get the feeling we are constantly being watched and listened to?

Who's Watching?

There are cameras everywhere, including dash cams, cameras in malls, and just people with their iPhones ready to shoot and record. In China there are cameras on the streets everywhere. And they also make extensive use of facial recognition, snapping your handsome façade as you enter the country. This country is one of the three largest countries landwise, but if they are ever looking for you, they'll find you in fifteen minutes, even if you're scuba diving in the Yangtze. I'm sure even the fish are equipped with cameras.

Most of us shrug it all off, saying, "I have nothing to hide." I myself wouldn't be that humble about it, but we all say it. Then again, what will we say? I have yet to hear anyone say, "I'm not sure I want cameras all over watching me. After all, I'm a serial killer. My hero is Hannibal Lecter."

I was on a cruise once and I noticed that in the dining hall they close down different stations periodically. For example, they might cover the dessert area with a drape, and a subtle sign saying "closed!"

At the end of the cruise they showed a film depicting highlights of the cruise, and this short video included a couple of clips of guests approaching the dessert area, looking around, lifting the drape, grabbing a muffin, and darting away. One guy even had his wife standing behind him as a lookout while he committed the heist. She was blond and the scene reminded me of Bonnie and Clyde. I observed the video and cannot say I saw a getaway driver resembling Michael J. Pollard. I don't know if they were shamed in any way during the film broadcasts.

But I can say that there is little doubt that the Chinese know about the event. It all likely got transmitted and logged in their database housing information about corrupt people. If these cruisers ever visit China, I can just see them sauntering along the Great Wall, when out of nowhere they get approached by two security officers in civvies who ask them to open their bag as they've been under surveillance for a while and now the suspicion of the authorities has been validated by a beagle trained to sniff for contraband muffins. In China they take corruption seriously.

Who's Listening?

In addition to being watched, we are being listened to, of course. Our cell phones are never far from us. Do you think Siri answers all our questions instantly out of the kindness of her heart? I wouldn't exactly nominate her for the Mother Teresa Humanitarian Award. I'm sure if you'd ask her what she thought about this possibility, she'd probably lie: "Oh, I do deserve this award. Did you know I spent five years comforting lepers in Calcutta?"

And let's not forget Alexa. You ask that little black box Alexa Echo to play some Mozart and you get the best of Wolfgang Amadeus piped into your room for free. But is she listening to our conversations? I once chatted with my wife about El Paso, Texas, and within minutes we Googled something and there were ads about where to get the best deals on ten-gallon hats in El Paso. I suspected mischief and so I immediately unplugged Alexa. Had I not done so, I'm certain Alexa would have interrupted Mozart's *Eine Kleine Nachtmusik* and hit us with a rendition of "The Yellow Rose of Texas."

And I'm sure all of this is known to the Chinese. I'd be a fool to try to enter China wearing a ten-gallon hat.

Spammers and Scammers: These Days

In addition, of course, to our losing our privacy, we have to deal with a barrage of spammers and scammers. Spam/scam calls? I presume I am not the only person getting them almost daily. Ever notice they come from a number of recurring sources?

Firstly, there is that annoying duct-cleaning call. This is usually from a guy with a thick accent. I just know the guy has concerns about the state of my ducts as he starts the call with "How are you this evening." This salutation gives it away—the duct-cleaning pitch is just around the corner, as does the fact that the call is always in the evening in the midst of our having our supper. I suppose these guys presume that while enjoying a fine fish delicacy, we are most fertile to his call as we say to ourselves, "Great Chilean sea bass. I'd enjoy it more if our ducts were cleaned."

He tells us that his company just happens to be in the neighbourhood this week and that this offer is the deal of the century. I am actually sympathetic to this guy as I gather from the conversation and the phone number on the call display that he probably lives in a country where he earns about $1.75 per day. Chances are high he may not know what a duct is as his own house probably does not have any. I end the call with a polite "no thank you."

Then there is the survey call. I instantly recognize this call because the caller starts off saying he or she will not be selling me anything. The subject matter is generally consumer oriented. The first question will be something innocuous like, "Do you own a broom?"

I stop there as I know where this is leading. If I say yes, they will likely tell me I am eligible to receive one week at some place like the ten-star Marriott Resort in Bali, all in for $39.99. I have a good nose for mischief. I therefore respond, "No broom. Goodbye." Still polite.

At least the duct and survey guys are not threatening, unlike that "Tax Department" scammer. This rogue, on a recorded message, admonishes you to respond ASAP or you will be arrested by the RCMP. I guess some victims fall for this one, figuring if they don't cough up money, they'll soon see two officers in scarlet tunics trot up to their house on fine black stallions.

And to add insult to injury, if a victim does pay them some money, he or she cannot offset it later against any taxes they actually do owe to the CRA. I doubt even H&R Block will tell you there is a provision in the *Income Tax Act* for a credit for "taxes" paid to a scammer.

Then again, it occurred to me that maybe they are actually benevolent reverse scammers. Just maybe, can it be that there is some eccentric gazillionaire behind it all who actually wants to give away money to whomever plays along? I can imagine if you get back to them you'll reach a live person who says something like, "Oh, thanks for calling back. Because you trusted us, our benefactor, Billy Buffet, will be sending you a certified cheque for one million dollars—tax free." It doesn't hurt to imagine.

But more dangerous than the "CRA" caller is the hacker. The caller tells you something like there is an error with your Microsoft software and that you're in luck; he will fix it for you now.

I have played along with this guy in the past. He'll ask if I'm on my computer now, and I say, "Yes, let's go." I don't know if that's wise, as in retrospect I wonder whether he can glean any valuable information by my just sitting in my kitchen over a green tea. I'd hate to think that he's in cahoots with the likes of nearby Alexa or Siri. I have long suspected these ladies of spying on us. They're modern-day Mata Haris.

Finally, there is that frequent mysterious Chinese call. I can't say too much here. It's always a female voice recording all in Chinese. I usually hang up after about ten seconds. Actually, I don't know why I still listen to the whole ten seconds or so. It's not as if my Mandarin gets any better after the first two seconds. No clue what she wants. But if she has a team of duct cleaners in the area this week, she isn't making her sales pitch easy.

I don't know how to stop these calls. If anybody does, please share this info with us. I even filed my phone numbers with the National Do Not Call List. I'm not sure if that will help. I realize it may eliminate my chances of getting that million-dollar windfall from Billy Buffet, but I'll take my chances on that one.

Spammers and Scammers: The Good Old Days

I'm not saying there were no scammers when we were growing up. They were different, more rudimentary, not tech driven. A popular one was the magazine contest. Some local guy would call you. They didn't have offshore in the '50s and '60s. He wouldn't ask how you're doing today. He'd tell you that you will win a prize if you correctly answer a skill-testing question. Given that we had nothing to lose by continuing, we'd OK him to posing the question. We expected a real skill-testing question, say, historical, as in how was Julius Caesar assassinated? The question was a lot simpler than that. It was, as I recall, "Can you unscramble the following four letters and come up with the name of a famous comedian?" The letters were, "o, h, e, p."

For boomers and their parents in the '50s and '60s, unless they lived with some still-to-be-discovered tribe in the Amazon, they would shout out, "Hope! Bob Hope."

The caller would congratulate you, saying you were a genius as most people he called couldn't answer the question. He made it sound as though you were an Einstein. While speaking to him I felt like telling him I also knew about E = mc2.

He continued telling you that you won a subscription to *Life* magazine. While you were patting yourself on the back, he'd tell you the subscription is for thirty days. But if you act now, you will also get one-year subscriptions for *Time*, *Readers Digest*, and *TV Guide*, all for $2.99/ month. And he'd add that with the knowledge we'd pick up reading these publications, we'd reach an even higher level of intelligence. I could certainly see how reading *TV Guide* could do that.

If you bit, the outfit would send someone over to your house with a contract for you to sign as he picked up your cash or cheque. I never actually read one of those contracts, but I heard they were draconian, tying you up for more than one year and allowing them to fiddle with the prices. There was little or no consumer protection legislation in those days. You didn't even have an out if you confessed later that you screwed up the contest and you accidentally said "Hope" when you meant to say Ed Sullivan.

And from what I heard, if you stopped paying you would get a letter from a "lawyer" demanding within seven days the $2.99 plus $10 for the cost of the lawyer's letter. (And no, it was not the lure of this lavish legal fee that encouraged me to go to law school.)

Another scam was the book club. You would see ads for these clubs in, you guessed it, the magazines. This was a slippery slope indeed. The ad would read something like, "For 99 cents, we'll send you three classic books of your choice from this list." The smaller print noted something like you then became "a member of the Book of the Month Club for life." You now had to continue buying books monthly until whichever comes first, your ninety-fifth birthday or the arrival of the Messiah.

I actually bit into this one at the tender age of about eleven. For my 99 cents they sent me three classics, such as *The Count of Monte Christo*, *Les Misérables*, and *Hansel and Gretel*. I recall the books were of ridiculously poor paper quality. The paper must have been made from tossed out desk ink blotters.

I read the books in part and decided to opt out. This, it seems, was not possible. I lived in Montreal and I soon started getting threatening letters from this company in Toronto. One of them said if I don't continue paying, I'll go to jail. This did scare me a bit as I recalled that Edmond Dantès, aka the Count of Monte Christo, spent fourteen years imprisoned at the infamous Château d'If off the coast of Marseille.

For that matter, *Les Misérables'* Jean Valjean got sent to the slammer for twenty years for stealing a loaf of bread.

I took these threats somewhat seriously. This was Quebec, where French law prevailed. Nor would I have felt better had I lived in Ontario and been threatened with the British equivalent of being exiled to Australia. The stress was too much!

I couldn't really show these letters to my parents as they didn't read English. Eventually I discussed the matter with my next-door neighbour, who was a teacher. She was helpful. She sent these goons a letter telling them I was an eleven-year-old kid and penniless, and asking them to drop the matter, reminding them that one of my three choices after all had been *Hansel and Gretel*.

The Toronto goons eventually backed off, demanding that we return the three books by post. With my good neighbour's help, we went to the post office and shipped them back. The French-Canadian clerk at the post office noted the package and the Toronto address and said, "You too, my frien'. Maudits Anglais." I'll save you Googling the word "maudits." It doesn't mean "nice."

As you can see, scammers are nothing new. As boomers, we experienced the joys from live people and on paper (or whatever those books were made from). Now we get it neatly online, from robots, with the stakes being higher. *Plus* ça *change.*

My Boomer Struggles with Technology as a Lawyer

Technophobia greatly impacted my working life. I experienced resistance to change because I was a boomer and a member of a very conservative profession that does not readily embrace change. The local courthouse law library even still had a book on its shelf called *Oliphant on the Law of Horses*, 1908 edition. I don't know if too many lawyers checked it out, and I really doubt there was a long waitlist to borrow it. I also doubt if you did borrow it and failed to return it by its due date, that you'd get a nasty call from the librarian saying something like, "Hey, how selfish can you be."

Fast forward to 1974, I was called to the bar of the province of Ontario (Canada, eh!). Initially, I practised in association with several other lawyers. I was the youngest in the group. The mainstay tool in a law office in the mid-1970s B.C. (before computers) was the typewriter. If your assistant made an error, she (probably 99% of assistants then were "she") would take out a little bottle of whiteout and dab it onto the paper, wait a few seconds for it to dry, and then type the correct character(s) over the white area. We had no problems with this delete function.

Then the magic invention came along: the IBM Selectric typewriter with auto correction. If you made a typo, you just back spaced, hit a correction button, and that would trigger a whiteout ribbon to delete the letters or words non grata. This awesome device likely rivalled the invention of the Gutenberg press. Imagine all the time we'd save. We might even be able to work with fewer assistants.

I was the first lawyer, as expected, in the office to get one of these amazing machines. The older lawyers were skeptical, lining up to pray facing the direction of the grave of Charles Holland Duell. (Y'all remember who he was!)

The cost, if I recall, in 1974 was about $1,000. (OK, they were Canadian dollars, but hard-earned.)

I recall the day the IBM guy delivered the machine. The entire office gathered around him as he uncrated and tested it. The event looked like a scene out of that historic moment in 1903 at Kitty Hawk. "Orville Wright" typed a few words and deliberately misspelled the word "banana," adding an extra *n* in the middle. With a devilish smile, he back tracked, deleted the word with seven keystrokes, and retyped it without the offensive extra *n*. Everyone in the room uttered a loud "aah."

One of the older lawyers there, Simon, was very skeptical, doubting it was happening and suspiciously observing the IBM guy. I waited for Simon to leave and return with some firewood and shout out, "Don't believe it. It's a trick. He's a witch."

Computers did not start hitting law offices en masse until the mid-1980s. Many lawyers thought that they would replace staff, such as assistants, still also known in those days as secretaries.

Given that the typing skills of most lawyers (including me) were not up to the challenge; that was not an option. We would just hover around our assistants watching with awe how they moved words around or redid pages of script in seconds.

By the way, we did not experience a mob of secretaries gone Luddite, attacking our computers with pitchforks.

There was no internet then. If you wanted to look up a word, you opened a book with a name like *Oxford Dictionary* or *Roget's Thesaurus* to find a suitable synonym or antonym. I was comfortable with that. So were many of my colleagues. In fact, I still have my dog-eared copy of *Roget's Thesaurus*, which I bought for 35 cents in 1959 at the suggestion of my grade 6 teacher.

Then came the turn of the twentieth century. Remember Y2K, where the doomsayers predicted all our computers would go bananas (spelled properly the first attempt)? As we entered the new century, I found practising law progressively more frustrating because of lightning-speed technology changes.

I would attend seminars, and one of the rages became the paperless office. The very thought of destroying paper never sat well with me. Although I see advantages of having quick access to reams of information, I like to have a document I can touch and spread on my desk and read, scribbling pencil notes, and making highlights with a yellow highlighter. As well, I was simply not able to fathom paying $2,500 for a medical legal report and then shredding it. I would find that blasphemous.

I found that the tech issues created a new dimension of dependence on an unlikely but not unusual source, common to my contemporaries: our children. The gen Xers. I found myself calling my kids for support on everything from what a browser was to how to clear a cache. And what a cache was.

My son Daniel, an insurance lawyer, incidentally, once visited New York. Being a great dad, I gave him a paper map of the city. He demonstrated his appreciation by unfolding it and saying facetiously:

"I am pressing my finger on 42nd Street. How come I am not getting a Google Street View?"

He went on to graciously decline my generous offer of the marked-up and colourful, yellow-highlighted, well-worn map that had served me well. Incidentally, I reviewed my will afterwards to make sure I wasn't leaving him my *Roget*.

The last few years of my practice saw the evolution of e-filing, e-discovery, e-this, and e-that. Even filing my annual application and report with my errors-and-omissions insurer had to be done online. I was always concerned what would happen if while fumbling through the process I made errors. Not a great way to impress my errors-and-omissions insurer. Might raise red flags.

The last year of my practice saw me attending a conference whereby a young trial lawyer (who looked as though he had just finished his freshman year at law school) told his audience that when he conducts a jury trial, he has all the proposed evidence on a computer, demonstrating it on a projector. In court, he hands out iPads to opposing counsel, the judge, the witness, the court registrar, and the jury members. I was knocked off my feet. I did, however, say to myself that likely the expense for all these iPads was probably less than the cost of my IBM Selectric.

He was adamant that he was getting super results, and that anyone not practising this way was in the horse-and-buggy age, looking for trouble. I mentioned this to my smart-ass son, and he asked me who my blacksmith was. (I guess he won't be looking for a copy of *Oliphant on Horses*.)

There are, of course, other stressors in the practice of law. But we lawyers are not the quickest group to adapt to change. I likely fell in the middle of the bell curve on this one.

This is a different bell from the telephone system companies. Though tempted, I will not go there, other than to say that when push-button phones came into being and we would call a number and get a voice that said: "And if you have a dial phone, please stay on the line," I stayed on the line. At least that led to having a chat with a live person.

Anybody getting the feeling that I and many boomers are not crazy about tech changes?

Webinar on Stress Gone Stressful

They are simply stressful. As a devout baby boomer I feel marginalized dealing with computers and other machines. I find it impersonal, frightening, and just overwhelming. I'm suspicious about spams, scams, and, especially, snooping.

Recently, while Googling something, I muttered under my breath that technology was stressing me out. By chance, I received an email about a free webinar on how to smash stress. Then again, maybe it wasn't by chance; maybe Alexa ratted on me.

I had nothing to lose. Unbeknownst to me, I would however have to undergo the ordeal and run the gauntlet of figuring out how to log in successfully.

I signed on and received an email suggesting three ways of signing in: (1) on my computer, (2) on a mobile device via an "easy-to-download" app, or (3) via telephone by calling some bizarre area code.

Apps do not sit well with me as I am never able to readily enter the right password. I'm certain Apple is out to get me. I get a note asking, "forgot your password?" but I don't see an option to say, "No I did not forget; I am entering it correctly. You guys are jerking me around."

Regarding the phone, I am not comfortable dialing these odd-ball 900 numbers for fear of reaching some scam telephone sex outfit following which I get billed $800. That for sure would stress me. And my marriage. Too stressful.

I clicked on a link on my PC, but I got lost. Firstly, I had to confirm I was not a robot. What bothered me most was that I was probably dealing with a robot here and I had to prove I was not one of him. I got that checkerboard test, this time showing a street scene and asking me to tick off all images displaying a bus. I checked off three squares where I saw buses, and no go. I then randomly checked off a fourth square not showing a bus, and for some reason it worked. All I hit was a garage. I suppose that fourth bus must have pulled into that garage.

After sailing through this maze, I received a message suggesting proper computer specs were needed. It talked about Firefox, Explorer, and Chrome in a language totally foreign to me. I am sure Socrates must have used similar language, and that led to the State ordering him to drink that hemlock. Rightly so.

I just hit keys in front of me randomly. Eventually I scored, but audio access only. The speaker asked listeners to enter their names and residences in the "chat box." Unfortunately, I could not see a chat box, whatever that is. He rattled off welcomes, such as "welcome Gerald from Chicago," and "welcome Marlene from Edmonton," and "welcome Cookie from Cleveland. Hello Cookie."

I felt excluded. I shouted back, "What about Marcel from Toronto?" I thought perhaps Alexa would hear me and relay my message. No go.

I did see a note offering tech support. I had to email my problem. With great difficulty I restrained myself from using language I would not use in front of my grandchildren.

To my surprise, a live person, Raymond, telephoned me. He asked if he could take over my computer after realizing soon enough his instructions to me must have sounded like they were in Klingon. I gladly gave Raymond control. I started to feel much better.

I finally joined the webinar. The speaker was making useful comments such as, "Stress can be stressful." He then listed sure-fire ways of dealing with it. One was breathing—in then out. How could I have missed that one? I zealously made notes.

Another was changing your thought focus. If for example your boss tells you you're fired, think about something you can be grateful about, like a gorgeous sunset. Noted. This one could come in handy when you're driving through a blizzard in Ontario in January. Getting stressed? No problem. Just imagine some clown in Fort Myers enjoying the sunset.

The seminar concluded. I realized I must inoculate my mind against the stresses of technology. I'm not certain what the answer is. One thing for sure, I'm definitely not asking Google. Maybe I can get friendly with Raymond?

Now for a positive note. I want to take a moment and think about some of the simple inventions that don't much rival computers and i-this and e-that. But I do want to salute them as they have for the most part and still are of practical use. Moreover, if I don't do it, I doubt anyone else will pay homage to them.

Paying Homage to the Basics: The *Big* Seven

Over one hundred million people voted a while back to come up with a new list of world wonders, namely the New Seven Wonders of the World. These include man-made structures such as the Roman Coliseum, the Taj Mahal, and the Great Wall of China. While these structures are awesome, I believe we should reflect and focus on a different set of world-class wonders.

I am thinking about simple inventions that are inherent wonders in terms of cost, longevity, and utility. Never mind senseless structures or complicated machines. My list consists of items that have been around for ages but in my view their value has yet to be assailed or dislodged in the big scheme of things. Here they are:

1. The Pencil

This tool never lets you down. Keep one in your car if you need to make a quick note, and on a frigid arctic day, unlike a pen, the graphite will not freeze. And unlike a computer, you don't need updates, upgrades, or security. I have yet to use a pencil and suddenly a warning appears on my paper reading, "This message may be spam."

And certainly Siri can't listen in and yap. I haven't tried it yet, but I doubt if I start talking about hockey in front of my pencil, I'll hear a voice coming out saying, "Wayne Gretsky."

And if it doesn't write too well, just sharpen it with a 50-cent sharpener. Unlike your anal-retentive PC, to get it working again you never have to restart. Nor do you need customer support. You'll never see a pencil-user calling some 800 number and have some voice tell him, "push 1 if your eraser has fallen off."

The pencil—a friend indeed. And in a pinch it even makes a good Q-tip (the eraser end that is). But don't put it into your ear.

2. The Toilet Plunger

I can probably buy enough bathtubs to fill the Taj Mahal with all the plumbers' fees I have saved by using a five-dollar toilet plunger to unclog sinks and toilets. This stout yeoman will vanquish most clogs in seconds, saving you $100 plus (and ever rising) for the plumber just to ring your doorbell. I don't know the origin of this device. I have tried to find out the inventor's name, but he remains a mystery. Hitting "toilet-plunger inventor" on Google didn't do it.

The plumbing union probably harassed the guy, urging him to sell out the patent to them. When he persisted in refusing to sell, they probably surrounded his house and burnt a wooden monkey wrench on his lawn. I don't know whatever happened to him, but he likely died unknown and a pauper. Whoever the inventor was, I tip my hat to him.

And speaking of fire, the next awesome tool is:

3. The Match

Imagine how we take this item for granted. Kids nowadays figure the match has one purpose—to light a joint (legal in Canada). The cave-man would have been clubbing himself in awe were he to have been given a book of matches. If as some philosophers have said, the world is made out of wind, earth, water, and fire, then we have 25% of the world in the palm of our hands in a little matchbook that might read, "Joe's Delicatessen." These days the matchbook might also read something like, "www.joesdeli.com. But that's another story. We won't go there.

4. The Postage Stamp

Say all you want about the post office, the fact is that, at least in theory, if you put a nickels-and-dimes stamp on a letter in Montreal it will likely be delivered to its intended recipient in Kelowna, British Columbia, within a day or two. To send it to Sydney, Australia, you will have to put on about a dollar's worth of stamps, but within a couple of days it will sail by the Sydney Opera House and reach its destination.

True, postal service is not perfect. Sometimes it seems that that letter you are sending from Montreal to Kelowna or even to a neighbouring Montreal address has gone to that address via Sydney, Australia. In fact, I am starting to suspect more and more that this is the case. But in principle, the lowly postage stamp still does its job. And unlike emails, it will not bring you a virus. It can however bring you junk mail. If it does, you can take out your matchbook. Or try flushing it down the toilet (if you have a good plunger on hand).

5. The Post-it Note (aka the Stickie)

This is a newcomer in the scheme of things, but I find that the stickie is the greatest invention of the last quarter century. My office would have come to a complete standstill without the stickie. A day did not go by wherein I did not leave my assistant notes reading, "Please get Henry Wiggly in this week" or "I am going to Tim Hortons." Scratch-pad notes can move around, and emails may not arrive as instantaneously as we would like them to. But once you put a yellow stickie on your assistant's computer screen, it's there and she can't miss it. No way will she say, "Sorry, I didn't see it, my computer was down."

And they make great bookmarks too.

And there were some days where I did not ask her to get Henry Wiggly in. For that matter, I didn't even have a client called Henry Wiggly. I use his name to protect confidentiality. I don't know even who Henry Wiggly is. Maybe he is the guy who invented the toilet plunger. Who knows?

6. Deck of Playing Cards

I don't care how many video games you can load into your computer, the best game in town you can still hold in your hand, to wit, a box of playing cards. These fifty-two cards are as useful and ubiquitous as they were when we were growing up playing simple games such as War and Go Fish. And if you have nobody to play with, you can always play one of the dozens of varieties of Solitaire. A deck of cards takes playing with yourself to a new dimension. (That's as far as we'll go on Solitaire.)

Nor will cards raise the furor and excitement on an airplane that electronic devices do. I have yet to hear a flight attendant announcing, "Please put away all playing cards as playing poker can affect the aircraft's navigational system, causing it to stray to Cleveland."

A word of caution: Be careful not to bore people with those inane magic card tricks—especially people carrying matchboxes.

7. The Wheel

Yes, let's save the best for last. In my book this is still the greatest simple wonder of the world. This becomes even more evident when you start having increasing backaches. Every week I wheel my trash out in bins affixed with plastic wheels. This is sheer ecstasy. Well, maybe it's not quite ecstasy but it sure feels great.

And how many people do you see at airports these days with luggage sans wheels? Only the hearty macho travellers. Or the youthful backpackers. There are more. I am talking about the rest of us who often start our trips with luggage with wheels but when we get to our designations, the baggage handlers send them down the luggage carrousel with the wheels missing. But that's a different story.

Whenever I watch a construction worker moving a heap of dirt in a wheelbarrow, I feel like going over to him and asking him to offer his gratitude to the wheel and to say, "Thank you, wheel." I have yet to do that, fearing an undue response as in his previous job he may have been an Air Canada baggage handler.

Let us all pay homage to the simple, eternal, and inexpensive wonders of the world. Never mind the Taj Mahal, or the Coliseum. They would probably overflow and flood without a toilet plunger. Forget the latest Airbus or the Apple watch. Too complicated. Just take out your pencils and a stickie and write down these magnificent seven and say thank you. And after all, an attitude of gratitude is also supposed to bring happiness.

What Is Good about Technology? The Balanced Opinion

I have spent a fair bit of time and space squawking about the trials and tribulations of technology, from my boomer's lens. Fair enough. However, as I write, we are in the midst of the COVID-19 crisis and it is only fair and just and right to present a balanced perspective. And as I no longer practise law, I can afford, or rather, I am allowed to say good things about the other side, without retribution. However, firstly, let me take another jab at the bad.

The news. The media is out there 24/7 giving us instant updated news. My view is that too much of it is disturbing. I really don't think we all have to know how many people contacted the disease in Denmark in the past twelve hours, that nobody knows for sure how long this will continue, or that it's all the fault of ex-President Trump. We cannot do too much about this information. Full stop.

What would interest me would be a news item saying something like, "Hey, a perfect vaccine has just been developed. One shot only needed—100% effective. It will be delivered to your doctor's office by Tuesday. Hey, Strigberger, what are you waiting for? Call your doctor." OK, I'm easy. I don't expect that announcement. I can wait 'til Thursday.

So now, for what's good about technology these days, let's go back about one-hundred-plus years and talk Spanish flu. It killed millions around the world. Actually, I have a connection with this event. My former office. True. My office for my last thirteen years of practice was in a quasi-heritage house on Yonge Street in Thornhill, the area just north of Toronto. This township was established in the late 1700s. The house I practised in was built in the mid-1800s and it was occupied by a doctor. And then other doctors for a while. During the Spanish flu outbreak in 1918 it served as the main information centre for the outbreak in what was then known as York County.

If you wanted to know what was happening, you would go there and presumably someone would tell you what they could. I'm not sure if they were into social distancing at the time or if they wore masks. I did see some pictures of those days where some people wore them. I can say for sure when you got there, you were not greeted by a waiting bottle of Purell.

In this area, this house was your CNN, your Fox, your CP24. I suppose in 1918 not everyone even owned a radio. This pandemic lasted about three years, killing about 55,000 Canadians. This is just a bit less than the number of Canadians who lost their lives in World War I.

As an aside, I noted from an archive site that of the over 55,000 killed in the war, twenty-one were shot by firing squad, for desertion. I imagine if this were today, desertion in my view would or should encompass being distracted by your cellphone while the officer in charge is shouting out orders.

As for my office, the pandemic ended and eventually after a few turnarounds in ownership, a couple of lawyers bought the place and, as they say, the rest is history. When I moved in in 2003, I was not aware of the house's historical significance. Interestingly, from day one I always kept a bottle of hand Purell on my desk.

We have come a long way, tech-wise. The buzzword of the day is Zoom. Groups can actually meet in real time, compliments of Zoom and similar technology. We are being cautioned about security risks, including privacy issues. I'm not overly concerned. What can I lose if some hacker tunes in and sees me watching a lecture on revelations from Albert Einstein's barber?

Nor is Zoom perfect. We have all heard of accidental instances where unwanted sounds come out, or parties are seen smoking cigars or compromised seated comfortably in the smallest room in their house. And there was that Texas lawyer who appeared through video filters looking like a "puddy tat." Meow. At least he agreed he imported some humour, making lawyers appear more human.

Some parties have also been known to wear a jacket and tie but no pants. I wonder if Zoom were to become a new normal, the haberdashery industry would change and come up with one-piece suits. Would it adapt and follow suit? (No apology offered!)

They'd have to come with a caution: "**Warning**. This suit is for Zoom purposes only. Not designed for complete coverage. Remember not to wear by itself when leaving your house."

I am also visualizing that iconic lynch mob scene from *To Kill a Mockingbird*, where Atticus Finch (Gregory Peck) stands between the angry mob and his client, talking them out of storming the jailhouse.

Would that scene play out differently during a pandemic? A Zoom lynch mob?

MOB: Atticus Finch, hand over your client.

ATTICUS: Go home now, or I'll mute you all.

And I suppose spammers can also get into the game. It would not surprise me to get an email announcing a Zoom meeting of the International Association of Duct Cleaners. What would give away the scam is that they would say the meeting is taking place this week in my neighbourhood. Hey, technology is a double-edged sword.

Social media certainly helps mollify the scourges of our current isolation practices. You can instantly watch and learn how to fix your roof without falling off it, how to keep your kids busy without locking them out of the house, or how to make great pancakes, including how to make your own maple syrup if you run dry.

Had you run out of maple syrup in 1920, you would have had to go into the woods and look for a willing and sap-capable tree, risking getting discovered by a big black bear that was not into social distancing.

And thanx to the internet, we are all graced with tons of humour, which always lightens the load. My favourite piece so far is a cartoon depicting Waldo in a room with only a handful of people. The caption reads, "It's much easier to find Waldo now." Another favourite is the picture of a black dial phone with the caption reading, "If you ever used this device, you are COVID-19 high risk." Resonates with boomers? You can find others—after you finish reading this book, of course.

Technology does indeed make life easier and more fun. At times. Given that our forefathers of one hundred years ago didn't have a fraction of the know-how we now possess, and yet that pandemic came and went, we would expect and hope for this one to end quickly.

And we can all agree that Commissioner of the United States Patent office, from 1998 to 1901, Charles Holland Duell, who allegedly said in 1901, "Everything that can be invented has already been invented," was dead wrong. We're still waiting for some good stuff to 100% knock out COVID-19.

CHAPTER SIX

Perks and Prejudices:
A Balanced View, Naturally

Old age is a great time of life. You get to take advantage
of people, and you're not responsible for anything.
~ George Carlin

As we get older, or should I say "better," we experience a variety of perks and prejudices. Actually, the first thought that comes to mind is that maybe we don't really get better. At least physically. Maybe wiser. Probably wiser. And if we act wisely, we can best hold our own physically. So that is better.

Let's deal with the prejudices first. OK? OK boomer, that is. I have previously mentioned this 2019 comment being the brainchild of that age twenty-something New Zealand member of parliament who in response to a senior MP said, "OK boomer." This has become a derogatory phrase meaning, in short, "We hear you; now go back to your planet."

This expression became viral soon enough, and it unfortunately was followed shortly thereafter by another virus—something 19. One virus leads to another. It delineates the controversy and conflict between the boomers and the Generation Zs and millennials. Like I said earlier, at least we don't proudly call a small Starbucks coffee a "Grande."

All of which gets me back to one of my favourite authors, Mark Twain, whose perspective of the youth bears repeating: "When I was a boy of fourteen, my father was so ignorant I could hardly stand to have the old man around. But when I got to be twenty-one, I was astonished at how much the old man had learned in seven years."

Do these words still resonate? The younger generation has always been skeptical and critical of their older folk, and we elders have always suggested these wet-behind-the-ears spring chickens have a thing to learn from us, and they don't know how good they have it.

I'm sure these sentiments were readily rampant throughout history. Probably after Gutenberg invented the printing press, the younger set were the prime customers of printed products. The sons likely said to their dads, "Hey, old man. Want the news? Pick up a newspaper."

The father likely responded, "Don't interrupt me, Eric. I'm trying to listen to the town crier." I'll add that after this interruption the dads likely also boxed the kids' ears. Good for them.

And probably this natural generational rift was noticeable in biblical times. Do you think Noah enjoyed building that ark for over one hundred years by himself? He likely shouted at his sons many times to give him a hand. "Hey, Japheth. How many times do I have to ask you to put down that ball and pick up a saw? The great flood is coming in about sixty years."

And when it did arrive and all were aboard safely, I'll bet each of the three sons didn't stop bugging their dad to let him at the controls. "Hey, Dad, can I take the wheel?" Nothing changes. I'm sure the sons even blamed Noah for the climate change.

And I'll bet even the cavemen experienced intergenerational friction. Dad would say, "Hey, Zonk. The cave is running low on meat. Put down that paint brush, get your club out, and bring us back a brontosaurus."

I don't know what Zonk would have said, but I doubt he'd tell his dad that he should try eating plant-based. If he did, he'd likely get his ears boxed. And he'd deserve it. *Plus* ça *change*. There's nothing new under the sun. Nor the sun itself. Not even climate change.

I'll confess that in my non-golden years, I also had similar negative (and unwarranted) sentiments against older people. And the age bias is all relative.

While in our early twenties, my wife and I travelled through Europe by train. We were sitting in a compartment one day together with three other people of similar vintage and a slightly older gentleman. Actually, we didn't know how old he was, but he made us uncomfortable. We all thought, what's the railway doing letting this geezer occupy our compartment? Are they begging for a class-action lawsuit?

We were all curious about how old this guy was. All we knew was that he was a teacher from Wisconsin and that he was going to Zermatt, Switzerland. To determine his age, we decided to play a game and show one another our passports. This way we'd be able to take a peek at the old man's date of birth. Our ages were in the eighteen to twenty-four range. We took a sneak peek at his passport, and get this, he was thirty-three years old! Our suspicions were confirmed. The railway stuck us with this old fart. Ugh! Wait 'til they hear from our lawyers.

This trentigenarian told us at length about the beauty of Zermatt, suggesting we make sure we go there. Our collective response was, "Right, sir. Can't miss it." I'm sure we all had visions of a bunch of residents from a retirement home lined up one behind the other making their way up the Matterhorn pushing their walkers.

Isn't it all relative? To this day, Shoshana and I refer to anyone older who bores us with useless information as "Zermatt." Come to think of it, our reaction does sound a bit like "Hey, boomer." Guilty.

Some biases are a bit more subtle. I've noticed that when I'm on the phone with a younger person, he or she presumes that since I dared use the phone rather than go online, I am a fossil, and he'll say something like, "I can help you. Do you have a pencil and paper ready?"

I have a good idea what goes on in this guy's mind. I know he doesn't know what those tools even are. He's likely reading from a script. "Boomer on the line. They still use pencils and paper. Google same if you want to know what those archaic instruments are. See also 'dial phone.'"

This is especially so if I have to give them my date of birth. If I say 1947, I may as well say right after Columbus landed in America. I called a financial institution recently and the lady asked me my date of birth, followed by my telephone password. I hesitated for a second to take a breath, following which I said, "Giraffe." She gave me an exuberant cheer, the likes of which would be reserved for a superstar athlete like Serena Williams. I just visualized the agent giving me a high five for remembering giraffe. By the way, regarding the telephone password, if you are a hacker, "Giraffe" is a random name, not my mother's maiden name.

And if you do get on the computer, they start to patronize you. They'll ask you to key in some bank website and when you do, they'll offer disproportional praise. "Ah, you're at the sign-in page, excellent!" I'm sure the bank person is comfortable and sincere in giving me this superlative score.

It gets worse for even older people. I visited my late mother at a retirement home once, and the residents were playing Bingo. One lady had a caregiver next to her who really piled it on. "Wow, Miriam. O-62. You placed the chip on the right number. Now only twenty-one more numbers to go 'til you fill your card. Awesome."

I'm all for positive feedback and reinforcement, but placing a Bingo marker successfully does not warrant praise that might be accorded the discovery of the ultimate COVID-19 vaccine.

There are of course real perks on the table when you hit senior status. A lady of this vintage whom I ran into on a cruise while sipping an espresso said in her wisdom, "Life begins when the kids are out of the house and the dog is dead."

Although there is some comfort in the reduction of responsibilities, I really still do miss my beagle. And there are other pluses in hitting these golden years. One is the "senior discounts." So if you go to a movie theatre or a hotel or a zoo, you get a "senior's discount." Of interest is that the magic qualifying age is around sixty-five. I note that since I hit the late fifties, somewhere, nobody ever asked to see my ID to confirm I am over sixty-five. I guess the young ticket seller takes one look at someone showing some aging and says to herself, "Here's another geezer."

I will say I was asked for my ID in Texas a few times when I tried to buy some beer at a supermarket. The register clerk, likely under twenty-one, wanted me to prove I was over twenty-one. He said that was the law. I reminded him I was old enough to be his father, maybe even his grandfather. He insisted if I cannot satisfy him that I am over twenty-one, no beer for me.

To convince him of my vintage, I uttered the words, "typewriter," "record player," "Howdy Doody." He looked at me as if I came from the planet Zargon. I expected him to go into the parking lot and look for my flying saucer.

I did not say anymore as I recalled that Texas had the highest state rate of executions. I did ponder if having to show ID to prove you're over twenty-one was the law or not in San Antonio. I wondered whether he was being deliberately difficult as I was of a person in his golden years. Something like when we were back on that train with Zermatt.

I agreed to show him my Ontario driver's licence. I asked him if it proved beyond a reasonable doubt that I was over twenty-one, could we hug one another. He agreed. And when I opened my wallet to display the satisfactory proof that I was not still in my teens, he never looked at it. He just proceeded to give me a hug. All good. An unexpected perk. This cordial event happened of course in the year 2017 BC (before corona). I'm not sure we'd bond this way going forward.

I also note most places will give discounts to "seniors and children." I don't know if this linkage is a positive or a negative. I once again think about Shakespeare's seven stages of man, and I see he does not display much stock for either children or seniors. They have their entrances and their exits. And he does call the last stage "second childishness." It's almost as if these discount notices at the movie theatres are saying, "You guys are pathetic. Here's 10% off. Enjoy the popcorn."

Speaking of exits, I shall be discussing longevity and death shortly. Stay tuned. No rush. But before death, we generally do something else.

CHAPTER SEVEN

The *R* Word: Retirement ... Ready?

I've reached an age when, if someone tells me
to wear socks, I don't have to.
~ Albert Einstein

"A re you retired yet?" This was the most common question people would ask me as I drifted into my mid-sixties. The second most common question was, "Oh yeah, then when are you retiring?"

I stopped practising law in early 2017. I have since been focusing on my ongoing humour writing and speaking endeavours.

This leads me to the third most common comment, "Lawyer and humour? Isn't that an oxymoron?" (It's good to know what the public thinks about lawyers. But that's a different story.)

How and why, you ask, did I retire, or perhaps transition? Ah huh!

Non-retirement Retirement

A little history is in order. The Big Bang of both careers started one afternoon in grade 2 when my mother took me to my physician. Upon arrival, his receptionist said he was ill. When I got to my class late, the teacher asked where I had been. Innocently, I replied, "I went to the doctor, but the doctor was sick."

The kids broke out in uncontrollable laughter. After all, doctors do not get sick. They're "the doctor." They're superhuman. I felt exhilarated by the laughter. It was a magic lotus-like elixir.

But the teacher was not amused. She said, "Trying to be funny?" She punished me. I had to write out twenty times, "I will not joke around."

I thought that was unfair. There and then my law career started. Sort of. I wanted to pursue fairness passionately. But what profession deals with justice? At age seven I had never heard of lawyers.

That laughter buzz stayed with me and I became the class clown. On one occasion, another teacher, who thought I was a bit eccentric, said to me, "You should go with your mother to a psychiatrist." I responded, "What's wrong with my mother?" That comment got me ejected from the class. The injustices continued. But the ensuing laughter from my classmates was well worth the consequences.

Not long after, *Perry Mason* came along on television. I was enthralled by his character. People are accused of a crime they did not commit, they hire a lawyer, and he proves they're innocent. I'm in. I'll show those teachers.

Near the end of my undergrad years at McGill University, I realized my career path was a toss-up between law school and the comedy world. I loved both options but felt I had to focus on one. Comedy it was.

I took a year off and freelanced for the CBC and others. I also applied to law school in the unlikely event I could not make a living freelance writing. The unlikely event became likely. I got called to the Bar of Ontario in March 1974.

My passion for comedy and humour, however, was unabated. I contributed stuff for publications, legal and non, including the *Toronto Star* and the *Globe and Mail*. As well I published my first book, *Birth, Death and Other Trivialities: A Humorous Philosophical Look at the Human Condition.*

In the late seventies, Yuk Yuks and other comedy clubs came along, and I spent several years having the time of my life doing stand-up, sharing the stage with the likes of unknown comics such as Howie Mandel, Bob Saget, and Jim Carrey. I was tempted to move down to LA, as they did, and take my chances, but I did not think my good wife and three small kids would appreciate me closing my practice and risking financial ruin. This was not my idea of early retirement.

I did do various gigs, including a most memorable appearance at a conference of the Ontario Superior Court of Judges' Association. This was the first time any judge reacted to my presentation with applause (it was also the last time). I experienced that grade 2 buzz-moment feeling, big time. And I even got paid for it (as opposed to being made to write out some nasty sentence twenty times).

But a litigation and divorce law practice can tax your time and nerves. We have good days and bad days. I was indeed making justice happen on the good days. But the bad days kept me up in the middle of the night, ruminating about my cases and concurrently lamenting that they kept me from freely pursuing my labour of love, namely bringing humour to the planet.

As I was nearing age seventy, I thought about that adage, the best time to plant an oak tree is twenty years ago. The second-best time is today.

Was age an issue? I thought about some late bloomers. I noted that Winston Churchill became PM, hitting the big time at age sixty-six. And Colonel Harland Sanders sold his first franchise while in his sixties. Even Stalin reached his prime as a senior.

And let's not forget Moses, who while looking for a stray sheep on Mount Sinai at age eighty got called into action via a burning bush message to return to Egypt and tell Pharaoh to let his people go. This event was probably history's first command performance.

As we know, Pharaoh did not listen to Moses. I wonder if the reason for this intransigence was perhaps the age gap between Moses and Pharaoh. Could it be that it was like a boomer negotiating with a millennial?

Moses: Pharaoh, let my people go.

Pharaoh: OK old man.

Moses: Is that a yes?

Pharaoh: Right. Dream on. I'll let them go when the Nile turns red.

Moses: Be careful what you wish for.

Fast forward a few plagues, like water turning to blood, hail and thunderstorms, and darkness, delivered by Moses.

Moses: Will you let them go now?

Pharaoh: OK, old man. Just stop this climate change.

I can't say it all unfolded this way, but who knows. Makes sense to me.

I, of course, had a different product to offer than Churchill—and certainly different than Stalin. Quite different. And at least my name wasn't Harland. Nor did I expect any special calls for a great cause for when I turn eighty. I'll be content passing on burning bushes and just collecting my Canada Pension.

But nearing age seventy, retirement slipped into the horizon as my number one son, Daniel, gave me subtle hints, such as, "Stop practising. You're old." I have since revised my will.

The emotional problem was making my announcement to friends and colleagues, and my most able and loyal assistant, Angela. (I can confidently say that now she can't hit me for a raise.) As for the logistics, fortunately Daniel was able to take over my clients. (He's back in my will.)

Since my practice termination, I have had the pleasure and leisure of launching my second book, *Poutine on the Orient Express: An Irreverent Look at Travel.* I am riding the star that came along that afternoon in grade 2, enjoying the ride and ready to go where it takes me for as long as my higher authority wants it to fly.

With some determination and much trepidation, I have indeed retired from my law practice. But I am not retired. I have planted that oak tree and I am nurturing it. Actually, what is retirement all about? What do retired people do?

The Bucket List: Visiting an Elephant Sanctuary and Other Must-Dos

In my view, the two key discussions of retirement are what you will do to spend your time, and finances. Health of course is a factor too, but this might be a bit harder to control, unless you can tell your body to behave. I have tried telling my prostate, for example, that a car trip of more than a half hour without having to look for a loo is sustainable. But it doesn't always listen.

So dealing with activities, what are some decent ways of spending your time? I suppose whatever works for you. People talk about that bucket list. For that matter why is it called a bucket list to start with? One theory is relating to execution. It goes back a couple of centuries when victims about to be hung would stand on a bucket, which they could kick away when ready. Hence also, the expression "kick the bucket." Having read that, I prefer not to call my list "bucket." And I'm certainly not ready to kick anything of the kind.

But when I Googled "bucket list," I got 686 million results. That's quite a list. I doubt anyone has on his bucket list the desire to read all these results. The sites on the first couple of pages look like lists themselves, as in "The 10 most common wishes," or "100 activities to get you started," or if you really believe you'll live to age 180, "1001 things to put on your bucket list."

They go all over the place. Some are outright risky, like bungee jumping. Or riding in a hot-air balloon. Or riding on a mechanical bull. These should be rightly labelled "Short-list bucket list." There should be a disclaimer saying, "Is your will up to date?" Not for me, thank you very much.

Others are weird, like visiting an elephant sanctuary. I suppose that's a place for retired elephants. The question then is, do retired elephants have a bucket list? Maybe they do. And maybe one suggestion for retired elephants is, visit humans in a home. "Hello, Mr. Rosenberg. Elmer is here to visit you. He says he knows you from your days at the circus." Question is, does Rosenberg also remember Elmer?

Then there are some items worth looking into that are safer, easy, and maybe even sustainable, which I never thought would be bucket-list items.

One is embracing your dark side. This one scares me a bit. When I hear dark side, some macabre thoughts come to mind; I visualize Lizzy Borden, hatchet in hand, paying a visit to her parents. Or I see Dracula the Impaler trimming some tree branches. Or even more intense, I see someone ordering a pizza with double anchovies. No, I'm not going there.

One I do like is to say something you always wanted to say but never dared to say. Easy. I'm strongly considering next time I'm in an Italian restaurant to go over to the server offering to sprinkle Parmesan cheese on people's dishes, and telling him, "This cheese wreaks. I cannot think of a viler odour on the planet. Toss it all into a radioactive-proof container and bury it ten feet deep. And when you're done, bring me another order of garlic bread."

And don't anybody say this item might also qualify as an embrace-your-dark-side item. I'm just trying to save the planet.

So as far as bucket lists go, you can select your websites from the 686 million, I'll select mine.

Sports and Games

But let me throw out some popular activities. Firstly, there are the sporting ones. Like golf. Disclaimer time: I don't golf. Nor do I consider it a sport. I know I'll probably rattle some boomer feathers, but being boomers, they'll understand. After all we're flexible, reasonable, and empathetic as most of our own parents generally never stepped on a golf course. They were too busy making a living and giving us a life.

I hear joining a golf club costs a fortune. Why would anybody pay thousands of dollars initiation dues, annual membership, and monthly restaurant and bar charges whether or not you use these facilities? And all this entitles you to experience vigorous exercise by riding around in a gold cart on miles of grass chasing a little white ball.

I'm not an exercise guru but I'm sure a round of eighteen-hole golf must burn at least eleven calories. It taxes the muscles for the foot to press on the gas pedal. And no doubt you burn a few more calories cursing and swearing when your ball lands in a sand trap. Then again, some, not many, golfers have the good sense to forego the golf cart and caddy their clubs on wheels. I respect these guys a bit more.

And many golfers take the game very seriously. I have seen golfers on a Florida course near the Everglades lose a ball in an adjacent body of water and stand at the edge trying to fish it out, notwithstanding warnings about the water being inhabited by alligators. I can understand jumping into a sand trap and trying to hit your way out. I'd doubt the probability is high of getting swarmed by red ants. But alligators are not finicky as to what they eat for lunch. And I doubt Alligator Al worries about the calories. And if you find yourself in the water with Al in hot pursuit, swim fast. Don't even talk to him about going plant based.

However, if golf floats your boat, do it. It's your retirement.

There is a relatively new sport on the block I have referred to called "pickleball." I have no clue how the name originated. And no, the ball is not green. This racquet game is a combo of tennis, badminton, and ping pong, and it has gained great interest lately. Florida is calling itself "Pickleball Paradise." Garden of Eden, move over.

I have never played it, but at least you exert some effort. And there is the social aspect as well as it is generally played in team pairs. Sounds OK to me, as long, of course, as you do not play at a court next to a suspicious-looking body of water. I'd keep my eyes out for a floating log that has two beady eyes sticking out, moves along towards the shore, and wears a bib.

Then there are the games, such as bridge. This game has eluded me since my college days, when a pretty classmate, Roxanne, I was chasing was an avid player who considered a guy's bridge skills as a major quality for accepting a date. My academic endeavours consumed much of my time, and I had little opportunity to properly learn the games and less opportunity to sit around in the common room where she and her line of suitors were busy blurting out strange chants like "three no trump."

I did, however, put bridge on my bucket list and resolved to learn the game, "one day." The one day came after I retired. My good wife and I signed up for a series of bridge lessons. That series lasted about three lessons. Forgive the pun, but it became abridged. I found there were too many rules, regulations, and conventions. And after living with rules, regulations, and conventions daily for over forty years, I just was not inclined to take on new ones.

It all sounded to me like you needed twelve points to open, but you couldn't do it if your partner did not have three diamonds in her hand, unless of course she was wearing a Montreal Canadiens hockey tuque. That part was obvious to me.

What really freaked me out was the instructor's apparent proficiency in the game. Without looking at our hands, he seemed to know what we had after we each tossed out about two cards. He would tell us we cannot complete the contract as we did not have enough tricks in spades. How did he come to this conclusion? I suspected he was in cahoots with Siri.

I have always taken completion of a contract seriously. No way was I going to be guilty of a breach. I quickly dropped bridge from my bucket list. I doubt I'll reconsider. More chance I'll go all out in that Italian restaurant and go postal against the Parmesan.

I don't know what ever became of Roxanne.

Travel? What's Travel?

Another popular obvious post-retirement activity is travel. But not as obvious as it sounds. This includes cruising, bus touring or private touring and the like, and snow birding—for the folks from normal places that have four seasons, one of which we are not crazy about. To a person living in places like Florida, "four seasons" means a famous musical composition by Antonio Vivaldi.

I can write a book about travel. Actually, I already did. And if you missed the plug a few pages back, here it is again, *Poutine on the Orient Express: An Irreverent Look at Travel*. Available on Amazon, etc. Plug done.

However, as I write these words we are in the midst of the COVID-19 pandemic. There is not too much travel taking place now. At least the book is funny. But assuming this too will pass, let me continue.

And just what is travel from the perspective of a boomer and up? Most of us are aware of the positive aspects of travel. Education, socializing, and just plain fun. Now that we know all of this, let me discuss the negativity coming from many baby boomers.

The big one I see is "procrastination." This is a killer deal-breaker in life generally, and it does not disappoint us as we get older and the issue of travel comes up. There are some common expressions people use that reveal this curse of the *P* word. One such phrase is "One day." One day we'll make that trip to Europe. You can be sure of that.

Ask them when, and they get more specific. "Soon." Does soon ever come? I suppose it does—soon. But not soon enough. Sometimes life gets in the way of travel, such as little pandemics, and that road not taken remains not taken.

Then there is the phrase I consider virtually obscene, and that is "We should." You know we should make that trip to France. We should take that Baltic cruise. We should visit the Rockies. They know they should, but they don't. We all know when and where they're going. The good thing is they agree they should. Maybe they actually will—one day—soon.

Then there are the patient optimists. They say, "Hey, of course we'll travel now that we're retired. No rush though. The sights aren't going away. After all, Morris, the pyramids have been around for thousands of years. They're not going anywhere."

All true. There is not too much risk of the pyramids disappearing. I doubt the Egyptian government will ever remove them and rezone the area for developments of condominiums. All windows offer a superb view of the desert.

I also doubt the pyramids will mysteriously disappear, though I would like to see the looks on the faces of these people were they to disappear. I don't know how they would react if one day they wake up and CNN announces, "This just in. It seems the pyramids of Egypt have disappeared. Witnesses noted shortly before the disappearance that a mummy wearing a top hat and waving a black wand, running around the area. Police have cordoned off all routes of exit. All tourists leaving Cairo should arrive at the airport earlier as they will be subject to secondary screening."

I suppose if this were to happen, the procrastinator would calmly say, "No problem. Everything happens for a reason. It wasn't meant to be. Maybe we will now travel to France instead. The Eiffel Tower isn't going anywhere soon." Like I said, they're patient optimists.

Then there are the people who want to travel and would travel but they are concerned about minor issues, such as health. For example, they may be afraid of getting sick in some remote foreign country. There is not much worse than falling sick or having an accident in some place where there is a scarcity of good doctors and they don't even speak English, other than motioning to you to open your mouth and say "ahh."

Or they may be afraid of possible security dangers. I have a friend who is paranoid, afraid of visiting places such as South America as he does not want to get caught up in a revolution. I can understand that part. But then again, this guy won't travel to most places, even in North America. I have put it to him saying, "Willy, when will you ever visit New York City? Not much chance of your sitting on the boat to the Statute of Liberty and it gets hijacked by rebels claiming Liberty Island." He has an excuse for everything. His learned answer is "Never mind."

And comfort and convenience and security may be issues too. When I travel, I like to be reassured that I am never too far from a clean washroom, a Wi-Fi–friendly zone, and a Costco. But I do knock myself out compromising my standards occasionally, not getting obsessed with the washroom or the Wi-Fi.

Another legitimate hurdle is the ability or inability to obtain travel insurance. It's certainly not a problem when you're younger. When my son Gabriel, in his thirties, wants to travel, he calls the CAA or the like and he gets one million dollars coverage for about $2.25/ day. Oh yes, he must answer a couple of health-related questions such as does your heart beat.

It's a different story when you hit the mid-fifties and up. We have been spending much of the winters in Florida. Our travel insurance application/questionnaire gets a bit pervasive. I can understand the first couple of questions, such as, "Has your doctor told you not to travel" or "Do you suffer from a terminal illness." Fair game. The insurer doesn't want to have to fund a crisis that is likely to happen, such as flying you back from Europe in the baggage compartment— and that will run them much more than that $25 or so per suitcase.

They would also incur the additional risk of the airline's losing you, as instead of flying you to Toronto, they ship you to Toledo. Could be either Spain or other similar-sounding "-do." I suppose you wouldn't care.

The bigger issue is coverage for pre-existing conditions. You need to be stable for a period, say six months. They have a few conditions defining stability, including not having seen a doctor for that issue or receiving a new medication or change in dosage for an existing one.

So supposedly if you are on blood-pressure medication and you visit your doctor and you get a couple of high readings, be careful. Monitor the doctor's words. Say you score a whopping 160/90, a bit high, and the doctor says "hmmm," butt in immediately and tell him, "I have plans for a Mediterranean cruise this summer. Don't write "hmmm" in your notes."

If you ever suffer a medical event and the insurance company requisitions your doctor's clinical notes and records, the adjuster will look at it and say, "Hmmm? This insured person was a basket case all along. When he applied for insurance, he never told us about that 'hmmm.' Misrepresentation. Claim denied."

But some people are simply not the travelling types. They may feel that after a trip you have nothing to show for it. It's true that when you return from a trip all you have is your luggage and your memories. And on a good day you don't import a cold or other bug. However, many people have a different bucket list, and they would rather spend their dollars on something material. I asked a friend of mine who rarely travelled if he would join us on a cruise. He graciously declined, saying he would rather spend the time and money painting his house. He noted that when I get off the ship, I'll have nothing to show for it and he, on the other hand, will have a freshly painted house.

Now I respect other people's opinions generally. I tried to step into his shoes and see it through his lenses, comparing the two decisions. I took a ten-day Mediterranean cruise, and he chose to paint his house. I suppose as he runs his paint roller along the walls, he looks at the sapphire blue paint and says to himself, "Looks just like the western Mediterranean. I'll add some grey and I'll virtually be able to see the Rock of Gibraltar. And unlike a cruise my foolish friend is taking, I'll have the entire trip right here permanently on my living room wall."

I don't know about that. I still can't empathize with the person who thinks this way, claiming when you travel you return empty-handed and that his choice of painting his house made more sense. I have yet to see a game show or contest where first prize is a barrel of blue latex. For two!

To each his own. If it floats your boat, do it. Pardon me, this guy isn't going on any boat.

Volunteering

Another commendable activity is volunteering for a community service. Hospitals and similar facilities are popular forums for volunteers. I noticed these people are often the first you run into at the facility. They are like the first responders. You might call them "first meeters."

I recall having the pleasure of having to undergo a colonoscopy, and I was wandering around like a zombie looking for the endoscopy clinic. My mind was a bit muddled and I couldn't focus on the unclear direction signs suggesting I follow the yellow line on the floor and then switch to the red one after passing the ob-gyn nursing station, ensuring that I veer left. Then again, I should not have been concerned about ending up at the wrong clinic, given the prize waiting for me at the colonoscopy place.

I was intercepted by an elderly volunteer who was cheerful and gracious. He held my hand, virtually, and led me to the right clinic. Given the joys of what was waiting for me, I was not sure whether I should have thanked him or blamed him.

These volunteers do have an important presence. And given that he was wearing a uniform and a tag, I ventured to ask him for a medical opinion. I asked, "Will this hurt?" The power of a uniform. And hey, any port in a storm.

Of course, there are numerous places to volunteer. By the way, I wondered whether a Walmart greeter is a volunteer or whether he gets paid. I Googled it and noted that they do, but you are talking very little, like $7 to $10 per hour. I have no clue who gets the $7 and who gets the $10. Does it depend on the greeter's talent? Somewhat like the pay scale of a professional athlete. You score those goals; you get paid more. Maybe Walmart starts them off on the low end and then gives them a rating and review. You greeted over 250 people in an hour last month. You set a record. You're in the majors now. Here's $7.25/hour.

Simply curious. Like I said, they're not really volunteers. Not for me. I'd sooner pull frightened people over to the colonoscopy clinic.

Loafing

Let me talk about a major perk about retirement—a super way to spend some of your time. Loafing! That's it. I often enjoy doing nothing. After almost forty-three years in the trenches, I have earned my loafing stripes. I don't have to think about which of three options to pick in a family law crisis that needs all my attention—now—to prevent Edna's nasty husband, Harvey, from kidnapping my client's child, Joshie, and whisking him out of the country.

Nor do I have to worry about deadlines and limitations, such as two years to sue someone, unless it's the government, which is six months, or a municipality where you must notify them within ten days of slipping on a wintery sidewalk or your case could be toast. Or should I say ice?

I don't have to worry about overhead, staff not showing up, or the Law Society breathing down my neck reminding me that lawyers are the custodians of ethical behaviour and that we must not even consider messing around with our clients' trust funds, or else. I just daily repeat my mantra, "I don't care; I'm retired."

When I feel like it, I go for a walk in the neighbourhood. In the autumn I love looking at the coloured leaves, stopping to soak it in for a few minutes, and saying to myself, "I can afford these minutes now. I don't have to rush to my office to deal with Harvey. I'm retired."

After soaking in that gorgeous fall foliage, I can proceed to the nearby Tim Hortons and have a medium black coffee and a maple-pecan Danish. And I can take my time sipping and nibbling. When I see people rushing about inside or at the drive-through, grabbing their stuff on the run, I say to myself, "What's the rush? I guess they're not retired. Too bad. I don't care. I'm retired."

And if I want to go to a movie theatre, I don't have to go in the evenings anymore. They actually have showings in the afternoons. They call them matinees. I vaguely recall doing matinees when I was a kid, on weekends. This is a real case of déjà vu. The movie theatres are a bit different now, I must say. Many consist of these mechanical sofa La-Z-Boy chairs, making the place look less like a theatre and more like a spa. If the movie bores you, you can easily drift off.

Speaking of which, at any time of day, if I feel like just taking a nap, consider it done. Forty winks it is. Hey, I don't care; I'm retired. And I certainly won't be dreaming about Edna's case.

People ask about how I spend the days of the week. The important question should be how I used to spend them? While in practice, I found myself stressing come Sunday evenings, knowing I had to get up Monday and jump into the lion's den, or perhaps the fire pit, or at times the ten-ring circus. I called the feeling the "Monday-morning blues." Near the end, I started getting the Monday-morning blues earlier on Sunday, and then progressively even earlier. Friday morning would arrive, and I'd feel good for a short while. Then I'd say to myself, "Hey, Sunday is only forty-eight hours away. That means Monday blues time will set in." What do I do about Joshie?

I soon developed a Friday midday blues syndrome. The only time it eased was if there was a statutory holiday falling on Monday. This helped a bit, advancing my Friday midday blues syndrome into Saturday.

Approaching age seventy is not a good time to be sad. I dreamed and longed for the opportunity to be able to just do nothing, little simple things, loaf. That dream materialized with my decision to let it go, to retire from practice. Had I not done so, I likely would have had the Monday-morning blues earlier on in the week, progressing from Fridays to Thursdays to Wednesdays, to Tuesdays, and then to Mondays. Come Monday, I likely would have worried about what's in store for me on the following Monday, next week. Who knows! Yech!

Now if it's a statutory holiday, I'll say something like, "Oh yes, Labour Day. I believe you don't work today. But come Tuesday…? And just as bad, for the kids, it's back to school. Hey, I don't care. I'm retired.

Now to have to get up on Monday morning is a nonissue. The blues days are gone. The days of the week don't matter. Sometimes I forget what day it is. I just know it ends with the suffix "day." That's all I must know.

The seven days of the week, once retired, remind me of the workings of the good Lord. On the first day, he created light. He saw that it was good. On the second day he separated the heavens from the earth. This was followed by creation of vegetation, the moon and the stars, birds, and fish, then land creatures, and so on and so forth, and on the sixth day he created Adam and Eve, the first humans. He told them to be fruitful and multiply. He said the same to the animals too. On the seventh day he rested.

I find that since retirement my days are somewhat similar. On the first day I open the drape in my bedroom and sunlight enters. I see that it is good. It is. I rest if I choose to. Optional.

On the second day I look at the heavens and the earth, if I wish, and see that they are good too. If all that looking and assessing makes me want to loaf, I do that too. A leisurely walk, and such.

On the next day, if I wish, I look at the sun, moon, and stars and say, "How pretty. No rush. Where's the Big Dipper again?"

I can and do follow my own schedule. I can munch on some of that vegetation in the form of a salad at lunch time, and I can now pick my own lunchtime. No clients in the waiting room. No affidavit to read through and respond to now. I'm sure little Joshie is in good hands. Or I can enjoy a larger meal at lunchtime or in the evening, as I please. I see that this is good. And I repeat the next day.

And as for those animals, as I stroll along the quiet streets of my suburban neighbourhood, I can greet people along the way, walking their dogs. And I can pat those poodles, retrievers, and beagles, as I please. All good.

As for the creation of Adam and Eve, I'm not a practising lawyer anymore so nobody expects me to do the impossible.

Of course I do think about my kids and grandchildren. I note that I was fruitful and multiplied. I note that my multiplying days are over. No problem. I can rest. Good time for a nap.

Just one matter before I take that nap. I am still a lawyer. Here comes the disclaimer. My comments about those deadlines or other legal notes are not to be considered legal advice or opinions. Do not rely on them. Get your own legal advice from a practising lawyer who cares about what day of the week it is, and who doesn't have the time and leisure to look at beautiful trees and sip a great cup of java and catch a midday snooze. And as far as the Law Society goes, I have not breached any confidentiality. Edna X is not my client's real name. Her real name was Amanda X. We're good. Anyways, I don't care. I'm retired.

Finances: Everything You Wanted to Know (Isn't Here)

How can we talk about retirement without discussing money? So let's do it.

Retirement means just that. You are retired from the workforce. This means that unless you worked pro bono, gratis, for free, you are not getting paid anymore. I will add that in some cases preretirement,

I did work pro bono, but this was not generally my original intention when I took on the case. But we won't go there.

The question now becomes how do you get along without the work money? Ah huh! The following info is not meant to be a financial guide. It's just my view of it all. If you want financial advice, you must read bestsellers like *The Wealthy Barber*. After all, if you can't get great advice from your barber, what is the world coming to?

You now must make do on your savings, investments, pensions, and so on, guarding it all from those scammers. Which brings me to the government.

In Canada we get the old age pension, or security, of about $600/month as I write. If we worked, we are also eligible for Canada Pension Plan (CPP) payments, which depend on how much you kicked in over those years at the grind wheel. The question is when you should start taking your CPP as you can do it once you hit age sixty, or you can defer it and earn lots more.

I don't know the exact numbers, but the noise about this choice sounds something like this. If you choose your CPP at age sixty, you'll get about $350 per month. If you hit it at age sixty-five, it rises to $847/month. If you're patient and not greedy and you hang in 'til age seventy-five, the Feds will give you about $4,567.47 per month (more or less). Of course, if you wait 'til you're ninety, I'm not sure I can add all those zeros here, but I can safely say you will grab the attention of the likes of Bill Gates. And Jeff Bezos of Amazon will approach you for a loan. As for the Canadian government, Parliament will have an emergency budget meeting to discuss cost cutting in view of imminent bankruptcy.

The government will have to sell the prime minister's official Ottawa residence at 24 Sussex Drive, and the PM will have to move into a condo. Most cataclysmic, the minister of finance, before announcing his budget, will have to forego buying that traditional new pair of shoes. Like I said, cataclysmic.

I don't know why it all rises like that, but I wonder if it has to do with compound interest. They call it "the magic of compound interest."

In short, what I have garnered is that if you invest $100 at a simple interest rate of say 5% per year, after one year you have $105. No problem. After two years if you remove that $5, leaving only the $100 there, you once again earn $5. *But* if you leave that interest there, it's $105 plus 5% on the $105, equaling $105.25, *and*, if you let it all grow and don't touch it over say twenty-five years, Bezos, move over.

Getting back to CPP, if you die before you start collecting, subject to some spousal survival eligibility, you're out of luck. You have left all that good money on the table. That Minister of Finance gets to wear those new shoes, not you. What you want to be able to do is get an idea of when you're going to kick that bucket (no further explanation needed) and then make an informed decision. Speaking of crystal balls, let me mention these financial-advisor gurus. Shortly.

In addition to these government pensions, some people are lucky enough to get pensions from their former employers. I consider this free money. Given that I was my own boss for my working life, I don't get a pension. For all of us who worked hard for themselves, this isn't fair.

I know many of these employees had a few coins deducted from their pay cheques over the years to help fund those pensions, but the employers generally kicked in the majority. All these guys can now comfortably retire. No clue how after a few decades the monthly take becomes so sizeable. Of course. Compound interest. It's all a trick. But it does look good now. It's amazing how when you're young you do not consider a company pension a benefit or perk.

A friend of mine started out as a public-school teacher in his twenties. I spent some vacation time working in a clothing store. We discussed perks, and I told him I got 50% off on clothing. He was envious, saying he did not have any perks. He did mention a pension, adding, "But that's not really a benefit. That's for old people."

Some forty-plus years later this guy is continuously getting piles of monthly free money. At least I still have that bright gold-colour paisley tie I got at 50% off.

How do you best sustain yourself financially once you are no longer working? My answer is, I don't know. I have read a bit here and there, and on a good day it is confusing and on a bad day it is confusing and inaccurate. I have learned one thing. The common denominator: The most important quality is to be able to see the future. If you can do that, you have it made. Your financial woes are over. This wisdom leads me to financial advisors.

Most financial advisors spew vital information you may not have heard, such as "The key to financial success is a good plan." Or "You need solid investments; success does not come overnight." Or "The trick is not to keep all your eggs in one basket. Diversify."

All sounds good to me, though the last one doesn't speak to me as I never once in my life collected eggs in a basket. That sounds like something Dorothy would have done. (Toto would have to get out first.)

They suggest we all run with these gems and wealth will be assured. Actually, I think about the cold calls I frequently get from financial advisors asking me for a few minutes of my time and telling me they can offer me a free portfolio review, and if I retain their services I am guaranteed riches rivalling those of Warren Buffett. I am sure this wizard of wealth exists, but I would not know how to spot him. Given that we all share this interest in successful wealth management, I have compiled a questionnaire to help my dear readers to determine whether you would recognize this ultimate in financial analysts, this prophet of profit, if you stumbled across him or her behind a *Wall Street Journal*. Please take a few moments to honestly complete the following quiz.

A. When looking for that mystical broker, you will try to spot him:

 1. walking on Wall Street

 2. walking on Bay Street

 3. walking on Lake Ontario

B. In trying to assess the broker's experience and credentials, you will want someone:

 1. who has worked in a large brokerage house

 2. who has worked in a not-so-large brokerage house

 3. who has worked in the land of Oz

C. Sometimes the name can be of assistance. In scanning your list of potentially right brokers, you would want a broker called:

 1. Douglas J. Richardson

 2. Nick the Greek

 3. Merlin

D. In listening to a series of financial gurus speaking at a seminar, you are most impressed by the one who tells you:

   1. of the imminent bear market

   2. of the imminent bull market

   3. of the imminent market of fishes and loaves

E. You would get most excited if your broker would drop by your office in the middle of the day and:

   1. buy you lunch

   2. offer you a martini

   3. wash your feet

F. You prefer an advisor who whenever he shakes your hand:

   1. squeezes it like a vice

   2. Looks you in the eyes

   3. reads your palm

G. The broker you are most apt to obey is the one who would tell you to:

   1. bring him a cheque

   2. bring him your umbrella

   3. bring him a great big pumpkin

H. You are most likely to vest your confidence in a broker who:

   1. rides around in a Cadillac

   2. rides around in a Volkswagen Beetle

   3. rides around on a carpet

I. You prefer to deal with a financial analyst who:

1. wears a three-piece suit

2. wears a tweed hat

3. wears stars and moons on his conical hat

If you answered numbers 1 or 2 to any of the above questions, then you may as well stay with your own financial advisor. You are where you should be. If you answered number 3 to all of the above, then congratulations; you'll spot him when the Messiah arrives. Meanwhile, hang on to your tweed hat.

But one more thing. At least loafing is free. Which gets us to the people who sometimes don't let us loaf leisurely. Family. They can be demanding.

CHAPTER EIGHT

Family: Go Forth and Multiply

There are only two things you can start without a plan: a riot and a family, for everything else you need a plan.

~ Groucho Marx

I would say that the most major rite of passage in life that ages you is when you create a next generation. That is, you have a child. Suddenly, as soon as the kid pops out and the nurse is cleaning the baby up, you have aged. Your actual age has nothing to do with it. This naked kid is now your responsibility, and by not doing much more than whelp a bit, he is saying, "Feed me, hold me, and I'm too small to fit on the potty; do something about it." And whatever he has in mind to do, it may just be in that nurse's arms. Afterwards, he's all yours.

I am fortunate to have three kids born four years apart. I can say that when number one son Daniel was born, I was twenty-seven years old. The twenty-seven number hovered in front of me, as if to say, "Hey, you're not a kid anymore. He is."

Four years later when Natalie was born, the number thirty-one looked a lot older than the previous number thirty. It talked to me, proclaiming, "You're a father of two kids now, Marcel. She comes first, though you can still enjoy some good things in life, like a chocolate fudgesicle."

When Gabriel came around, I was all of thirty-five. This was getting serious. Even older than that guy we met on the train, "Zermatt." While in the delivery room, my brain got busy and I recalled that Wolfgang Amadeus Mozart died at age thirty-five. I certainly wasn't entertaining the thought of death at the time, but then again, I doubt Mozart was. You might say I felt as though my aging system had taken a quantum leap. I certainly wasn't thinking about fudgesicles.

Here I was with a next-generation set of three. I recall hugging my father then. He was called Mr. Strigberger. Up until around then I was Marcel. It wasn't until I hit the mid-thirties that I heard someone say "Mr. Strigberger," I thought maybe they were addressing me. Just maybe.

The coming of the next generation dates and ages you. My kids would enjoy things like riding in an elevator, playing on a seesaw, or petting a pony at a fair, all while they laughed and giggled to their hearts' content. Oh, I found I could still share some of the kiddy pleasures too, though I was at times self-conscious about emitting hearty belly laughs in an elevator. I thought it might provoke some raised eyebrows. Then again as I think about it now, does it really matter? The process continues.

Grandchildren

And if having kids brings home the aging process to you, having grandchildren raises the bar a few notches. I hit that milestone in my late fifties when my first granddaughter, Leora, came around. In my excitement I called my assistant to give her the news of a birth, without telling her the gender, and jokingly she asked, "Are you a grandfather or a grandmother?" Unwittingly, in my excitement, I responded, "Grandmother. And she weighs seven pounds, four ounces."

And what is it to become a grandparent? From my personal experience I can only talk about being a grandfather. Firstly there is the title: "Grand." Isn't it really an oxymoron? By the time you achieve this status, unless your own kids are very passionate and fertile progenies, you are now well into your middle age. I recall getting senior discounts from Marriott after hitting fifty-five. By now a few of your faculties are already compromised. Just ask any millennial. OK?

The French similarly say "grand-père." Maybe the Italians have it right. They call a grandpa a "nonno." I wouldn't go that far, but I don't care to Google the term to find out its origin. Maybe it derives from a Latin word meaning "OK old gladiator. Get out of the Colosseum." At best it sounds like, "No, no, be careful and don't fall down."

Interestingly, the flattery continues, and the next generation of titles makes you a "great" grandfather. At this stage you just have to be old, at or nearing that Shakespearean last stage—that is, sans everything. It continues to "great-great." I'm sure that if you ever reach this stage, your calendar won't be too full; most likely your days of playing pickleball are done.

Although I may sound a bit cynical, it could very well be that some of our ancestors were great. Maybe I had a great-great-grandfather to the tenth exponential degree back in the Middle Ages who was a physician during the bubonic plague. Maybe he urged the people to wash their hands often. If so, they likely looked at him strangely and accused him of witchcraft. You never know. Now that I think about it, my hat goes off to him. He was truly a great-grandfather to the tenth exponential. I would have been proud of him.

But getting back to the present, although the term is flattering, "grand" is perhaps better suited for a large, magnificent piano.

Given that grandchildren and grandparents often, as the joke goes, unite against the parents, whom they view as the common enemy, maybe they should call grandparents something else. How about "better parents." That would make me a better father. I can live with that. It sounds more accurate than grandfather, and it's certainly more pleasing than "nonno."

Becoming a grandparent brings about changes in your lifestyle and mindset. I found myself thinking of the Bible, in that I begat X and X begat Y. I also thought of Shakespeare's seven stages of man, again. The good thing with grandchildren is that that mewling and puking baby doesn't do it in your arms anymore. It all belongs to your own kids. Revenge.

But history does repeat itself in ways. There is that déjà vu. As the grandchildren get a bit older, you start playing games with them. You realize it's been about forty years or so since you last threw a baseball. And for some reason, after a few tosses your shoulder aches. The kid, generally sympathetic and understanding, says, "More."

And when is the last time you played hide-and-seek? Exactly. The good thing is that at my age, and stage, I can still remember whom I am trying to seek.

We also find ourselves playing games like chess. The hardest part here was explaining to my grandson Nathan how the knight moves. And once I crossed that hurdle, I had to come up with an answer for "why?" I didn't know the answer to that one. But sure as hell I wasn't going to ask him to ask his dad.

Now that we have all this family, where do we live? Tip. Don't rely on your family.

CHAPTER NINE

Residences: The Elephant in the Condo

We gotta have a home.
~ Brook Benton, from "The Boll Weevil Song"

So where indeed do we live?

More Shakespeare: The Seven Stages of Residence

I have noticed that the bard's wisdom or folly can apply to the types of residences we go through in life. As according to Shakespeare, there are supposedly seven stages in man's life, I note that there are also seven residences as we move along. They do not fully correspond to everybody chronologically bang on to the bard's seven stages, but they are there.

The first is our parents' home. You start off there mewling and puking though not in the nurse's arms unless I suppose you're someone like Prince Harry. This home also includes the whining schoolboy, who creeps to school unwillingly like a snail, or at least as fast as his school bus takes him.

The second home comes around university time. Many students head off out of town and live in a university residence. At this stage, many take on Shakespeare's soldier's qualities in that they become bearded like the pard and full of strange oaths. Well, at least strange tattoos.

I myself never lived in a dorm as I went to my hometown McGill University in Montreal. I likely did not miss anything as in those days university residences were not co-ed. The women's residence was called Royal Victoria College (RVC), and no men were allowed near the place. Rumour had it that if a guy would manage to sneak in for a visit, he would have a better chance of surviving a stray venture into the Bermuda Triangle. The building was aptly named after that supposedly prudish monarch, whose stone statue still guards the front entrance. All the guys knew the place was impregnable and should they attempt an invasion, they would not have been amused.

If you haven't figured it out yet, this stage also corresponds to Shakespeare's lover stage. I certainly recall those days, as I would kiss a date goodnight on the staircase of the RVC, "sighing like a furnace," in front of Her Majesty's statue—Alas!

The third residence after graduation is usually the apartment. That makes sense. You get married, or not, and you find an apartment. Most of us do not return to our parents' house. Some do I suppose, and if so I'd call this "parents' house two." It's different this time. Your parents give you a strange look, like, "We thought we were rid of you." I count it as a third residence, an alternative to your own pad, though not generally a welcome one. Like I said earlier, when it comes to where to live, don't rely on family.

Residence four if you are fortunate, is a house. You're somewhat established, there is an income of sorts, and you finally live in your private castle. The castle comes with a good mortgage. We expect that. Speaking of which, I know that a man's home is his castle, but I never actually noticed whether those castles you see in the movies or read about in the literature ever had mortgages. I don't recall the Sheriff of Nottingham ever saying anything like, "Robin Hood ambushed and robbed my courier carrying this month's mortgage payment. How do I explain this to the bank?"

Residence number five is the turning point. The condo. At this point many of us find their kids have moved out (for good this time) and we are "empty nesters." I'm not crazy about this expression as it makes it sound as though the parents' presence in the nest doesn't count. The nest isn't empty at all. We're still there, quite relieved actually.

However, we are told a house is just too big for two people. Go into a condo. As an aside, one sad part about it is that by now your dog has likely passed on. Unlike that lady I met on the cruise—like I said, I do miss my beagle, Columbo.

As I write these words, I still live in my house of thirty-plus years. There are a number of reasons for this. Firstly, in a condo, though you do own property, you own your own unit but only an infinitesimal part of the common areas. A condo is great if you get ecstatic about being a 0.015% owner of the elevator.

Secondly, there are all the rules to follow. You can't change your flooring or stop your car where you want or have certain tradesmen attend without getting the consent of the management company. You even need their OK for that tradesman to use that elevator. Don't try telling him, "It's OK, I own 0.015% of it. It's mine. Trust me."

These rules are enforced by the management company, whose key person you have to deal with is often a tough woman who strangely is a perfect ringer for Nurse Ratchet. You might recall she was that no-nonsense nurse in the Jack Nicholson movie *One Flew Over the*

Cuckoo's Nest. I for one would never cross this lady as I would not want to enter the next residence with a lobotomy.

Then again, condo living has its positive sides, especially the potential for social contact (barring the odd pandemic). As well it has recreational amenities such as gyms and swimming pools (barring the odd pandemic). And of course, you don't have to worry about clearing snow off your driveway (pandemic or not).

But here is probably the main reason we don't want to move out of the house of thirty-plus years. We have too much accumulated stuff. This alone is a deal breaker, especially if one of the spouses is a bit of a hoarder, like Shoshana is. A bit. She has a narrow definition for what falls into the category of trash. Identifying a piece of garbage in our household is harder than spotting Waldo.

For example, we have this old wooden and wrought-iron bench sitting in front of our house. Some of the boards became detached and the bench became rickety, constituting a potential risk for any passerby who may be allured by it and seek respite. I was going to drag it out to the curb for garbage pickup. Suddenly my wife pounced out of nowhere and played guardian angel to that thing, putting her hand on it and saying she'll fix it. We dragged it into the garage, where it has been sitting in rehab for about a year. Whenever I ask about the progress of this restoration, I'm told, "It's on my to-do list." At least that potential passerby is safe from this potential bench quake.

Books are another item. We have so many books in our home I am considering hiring a librarian. And the value of some is a bit doubtful. One is called something like *One Hundred Years of British History, 1860 to 1960.* I'm not even sure how it got there. My guess is that we had a burglary in our home once and to add insult to injury, the burglar left it there. I certainly would not have bought it. The problem now is getting rid of it and similar junk books. Uh-huh. Verboten.

"You don't just throw away books," says she. Had I known this, I would have added to my insurance burglary claim form a claim for compensation for getting cluttered. I'd fill out that loss schedule, crossing out the word "loss" and adding "now stuck with."

We even have issues with food. My good wife of many decades has three designations for food handling:

1. The words "best before" mean "best before, more or less,"—KEEP;

2. Let's just continue watching those bubbles—KEEP; and

3. That isn't what it looks like. If you'd been a scientist, you never would have discovered penicillin—KEEP.

You hear people say if you did not use it for two years, you don't need it anymore. Given that we have been married about fifty years, and given that I want to maintain this matrimonial status, I shall not take that one any further. I will just say it's a good thing I'm not into dairy products. OK, OK, maybe I exaggerate a bit. Never mind about those bubbles. In any event, now you know why it's not that simple to just move out of that house.

The sixth residence is a retirement home. I am thinking of a formal retirement where you live among people your vintage who are still reasonably self-sufficient. It may look like a condo, but you don't own anything, not even a piece of that elevator. And unlike a condo, they provide some or all of your meals.

Many people would rather not go there as it is one step below a nursing home. But many people, especially snowbirds, without realizing it do live in similar milieus, such as those colonies, say, in

Florida. The places generally are restricted to persons over the age of say, fifty-five. Unlike a retirement residence, you are fully independent, and you deal with your own meals. However, there are subtle hints throughout that are meant to suggest that you are getting on in years, like the notices for social and recreational events. I can very much go for a walk at a clubhouse without having to see a bulletin for a meeting of Prostates Anonymous. OK, it's not quite like that but a notice of a pickleball tournament for survivors is close enough.

The seventh and final residence is the nursing home. I have indirect experience with this one. My own mother lived in one for seventeen days before they called me that fateful Monday morning to tell me to come over as it did not look good.

It didn't. Then again, neither did those seventeen days, when I would frequently visit and see a platoon of residents, mostly in wheel-chairs, sitting quietly or rambling on insensibly. I recall seeing a former university physics professor who kept on asking, "Where shall I sit?" Another gentleman was the former chief medical officer of a hospital who was led into a dining room by a care worker who held his hand like a nursery kid. Many of these people did not recognize their family visitors.

Shakespeare was right about this stage. I don't know about the "sans teeth" or "sans eyes" but there is no doubt about the "sans every-thing." I don't think even that boll weevil would want to end up here.

Sorry for the brief downer. I need a humour break now. Maybe I'll watch a Shakespearean comedy, or a Molière, or even better, a Seinfeld rerun.

CHAPTER TEN

Best for Last: Fear of Aging, Death, and Taxes

*It's not that I'm afraid to die. I just don't want
to be there when it happens.*
~ Woody Allen

Fear of aging-yikes!

Although I personally have not experienced it to a large degree, there is generally an uneasiness about aging. Nobody likes where this is heading. Shakespeare's last stage, "sans everything," does not exactly paint a picture of Arnold Schwarzenegger as the Terminator. Nobody wants to go there, but then again, nobody wants to die young either. We all crave that longevity (I shall get to this soon; it won't be long).

Although I can understand people being uncomfortable with aging, I have some difficulty understanding why many folks take steps to look younger. These bizarre actions include hair colouring, facial and other plastic surgery, and wearing younger-set clothing." After all, there must be a reason why as we age our hair turns grey. Take a wild guess. The reason is we're older. If dyeing our hair would reverse the aging process and increase longevity, that would be another matter. It would be interesting to see some hair sprays that would say on the label, "Apply weekly for one month. This will reverse your age by ten years. CAUTION: Using this product may result in your losing your seniors' discounts."

But alas, until this happens, all hair dyeing will simply result in a dark-haired person (still eligible for those discounts).

Then again, come to think of it, is there an ideal age? A baby? We'll never know what he thinks. A kid? They too bawl and complain. Teenagers? Young adults? Those were incredibly stressful times for me. I didn't have enough money, I always worried about upcoming school exams, and I was generally usually in love with some unattainable female. And as I noted earlier, I couldn't even accompany a date into the Royal Victoria College. Not good. And after I hit the forties, I started seeing doctors more often for normal coming-of-age conditions.

But I do have an answer to the question. I believe if you were to be able to stay at one age, the magic number would be thirty-nine.

After all, isn't this the popular age a lady, whose age you should never ask to start with, will respond with? This was also legendary comedian Jack Benny's stage age. At thirty-nine most of us are also reasonably well established. I was already for ten years the senior partner of my law firm. OK, I was a sole practitioner. Still.

At thirty-nine I was sans high blood pressure, sans multifocals, sans need to drive on a highway and after enjoying a fine large coffee have to desperately Google to find out where the next opportunity is to bail out.

Then again, we're all different and would we really want to stay frozen at one age? As I write I am thirty-seven, or rather, seventy-four years old. I can thank the good lord as I sit comfortably at my desk and write these words. And any chance I get, I'll find a reason to smile or laugh. Is this life to the fullest? Of course not. But it's certainly filled. I'll take it.

Longevity

You can live to be a hundred if you give up all things
that make you want to live to be a hundred.
~ Woody Allen

We boomers make up an exceptionally large segment of the population. The oldest guys now are hitting the mid-seventies. We hear phrases like "seventy is the new sixty" or maybe "the new fifty-five," or whatever it is. And whatever it is, most of us are concerned about the *L* word. Longevity. Although it's been a great trip so far for many of us, we'd like to stay on the ride much longer. There are a few longevity theories that always turn up, revolving around diet, exercise, stress management, spirituality, and genetics.

Much of this information is confusing or contradictory. For example, we hear that fish is good for you. I recall a story about some 106-year-old centenarian in Holland who attributed her longevity to eating a large piece of salted herring daily. Who can argue with her? Then again salted herring is loaded with sodium. The story did not mention blood pressure readings (hers, not the herring's).

I shall digress and say that we were driving through a country road in Holland once looking for a certain café. We came across a quite elderly looking lady walking along the roadside. She looked very much like the image I had of that 106-year-old centenarian, and I stopped the car and asked her for directions. Her answer was "Hello." Unfortunately, she didn't speak English. She did impress me, however, as she moved alone and unaided along the road. I wanted to ask her if there was a place nearby that sells salted herring. But my knowledge of Dutch failed me. Maybe I should add "learning Dutch" to my bucket list.

I now un-digress. I recall seeing a television commercial about yogurt. It showed these centenarian-looking shepherds, likely somewhere in rural Macedonia, gorging themselves on tubs of yogurt. They were apparently saying some words about how yogurt is the magic longevity elixir. From what I gathered, their message was that all you have to do is eat yogurt. They didn't speak in English.

If you ask me, I wonder whether this commercial told the whole truth. It would not surprise me if what they were really saying was, "Hey, Bogdan, enough is enough. Once that camera stops shooting, throw those hamburgers on the barbecue." I don't know. I do know I am not adding Macedonian lessons to my bucket list.

My only definitive contact with a centenarian was with Ben Sherman, of Toronto. He lived to age 105. He was the founder of a downtown hardware store. One day I happened to drop in and I saw Ben himself, sitting on a chair near the cash register, speaking to people. I didn't know anything about him, but I noticed some newspaper clippings on the wall about the gentleman's life. What caught my eye was a comment that every day he would have a shot of Canadian Club whiskey. This information got out and the whiskey company would reward Ben annually by shipping him a case on his birthday.

I felt honoured to meet him, and in chatting I asked if he ever worried about anything. His answer was, "I only worry whether that whiskey company will ever forget my birthday." Touché.

The largest centenarian population, or almost 60,000 of them, is in Japan, many being in the fishing villages of Okinawa. Research findings have attributed this longevity to a number of factors, including simple diets of grains, veggies, and fish; family care and involvement; spiritual activity; and stress management. This all makes sense.

As for the diet part, I have not researched to find out how many McDonalds or Taco Bells there are in those Okinawa villages. My intention is not to assail McDonalds or Taco Bells or other fast-food giants, but I do challenge them to run a commercial showing a handful of centenarians going through a drive-thru and ordering Big Macs and fries.

I am not sure what kind of fish those people in Okinawa are talking about. Can it be salted herring? For that matter, is there a problem with fish being contaminated with mercury? I don't know. And no, I am not adding Japanese lessons to my bucket list.

We can all see how family support can extend longevity. In addition to caring for their elders, the younger folk invite them to come along on those fishing boats and continue to engage meaningfully. They thrive on experiencing nature and contributing to the group.

While all this is commendable, I doubt we can apply and replicate all of these experiences for all callings in most situations. If I ever hit one hundred, although I'd like some involvement, I don't think I would feel empowered to come to my son Daniel's office and greet clients. Forget it. I don't care. I'm retired.

As I write, I am thinking about our monarch, Queen Elizabeth II. She is presently ninety-four years old. Her mother, the Queen Mother, died at age 101. I see some similarities with these two to the centenarians in Okinawa.

Regarding diet, I am certain that like those fishermen in Okinawa, the queen eats (and the queen mom ate) lots of grains, veggies, and fish. After all, re the latter, how can any Englishman or woman resist all those kippers?

And certainly there is that family care and involvement. Like those fishermen, the queen gets up every morning and she still has a job. Hey, she's Her Majesty. Gd bless. And just like those fishermen, where nobody really cares how many fish, they catch that day, I doubt the royal family, or others for that matter, really care how much work she gets done. If she ends up cutting a ribbon or two at a museum or just dusting off her crown, that's great. Or she is good to go for the day if she just sends an email or text or two to Meghan Markle and Prince Harry. The similarity to those Okinawan fisherman is inescapable.

Then there is the stress-management factor. This is vital. Those fishermen live a simple life, not stressing over much. They connect with nature and they are grateful.

The queen also lives a simple life. What, I ask, can be simpler than living in a humble abode such as Buckingham Palace? I am certain that notwithstanding its size, she doesn't spend more time keeping it clean than those Japanese fishermen spend fixing their nets.

The queen is also no doubt stress free. Given her great financial wealth, if she wants, she can probably buy all the fishing boats in Japan.

As for nature, she can visit her forests, and if she chooses, like other members of the royal family, she can join a fox hunt. I can't comment on the stress caused to the foxes. I'm sure they are not amused. Then again, at least the foxes don't get stressed worrying about Meghan and Harry.

And as the Japanese fisherman exercise pulling in those nets and unloading fish, the queen can achieve her daily exercise quota even if she just stands at a window in Buckingham Palace and does a royal wave. That'll burn up a few good calories.

Oh, by the way, in my rant about longevity, did I mention genetic factors? I think not. I suppose these matter somewhat as well. It is comforting that the queen mom lived to age 101. I have no clue how long the parents of any of those fishermen lived. Gd save the Queen.

My research did come across some centenarians of note. Firstly, biblically speaking there was Methuselah, who lived to the ripe old age of 968. I don't envy the guy. He must have spent a fortune in expenses paying for retirement homes. I read Genesis to find out what his occupation was. No luck. All I learned was that his dad was Enoch. Enoch died young, at age 365. Still not bad. Maybe Enoch and son were fishermen? (I'll mention Enoch again soon, in a different context. Promise.)

I note Methuselah died of climate change. He died in the year of the great flood. Nasty. Methuselah was actually the grandfather of Noah. Looks like Noah was nothing like those Japanese fishermen. He didn't provide that family care, failing to invite his grandfather into the ark. Shame on him! At least he didn't hunt down those two foxes in the ark.

But he himself did have many years, living to 950, being another 350 after the flood. Maybe one reason he lived a long time was that he worked hard as he was aging, taking over one hundred years to build that ark. That would certainly give him some exercise.

As for his diet, I don't know about those fish. Nowhere does it say that during the flood he would open a porthole and toss a hook line and sinker into the water. There certainly would not have been a problem with mercury contamination.

Another elderly centenarian was Adam, of Adam and Eve fame. He died young, compared to Noah. He lived just to 930 years. His diet? I'll guess fruit. Apples? Tree-of-knowledge fruit? Whatever it was it kept the doctor away.

There were some other notable centenarians who made the news this century. There was Monroe Isadore, who died in Arkansas at age 107 in a shootout with a SWAT team. Disturbing. I guess he didn't want to be arrested and risk getting hit with a life sentence. No chance of parole. Nasty.

Then there was William A. Del Monte. He was the last known survivor of the 1906 San Francisco earthquake, dying in a retirement home in 2016 at age 109. In my view, the earthquake probably left indelible emotional marks on him. He likely told the retirement-home people, "Make sure my room is on the main floor."

No indication that Del Monte was related to the canned-food outfit. Hopefully not, as this would get me back to the wisdom of eating canned fruit and make me reopen the discussion on Adam again.

There was also a handful of centenarians performing incredible athletic feats. One was Hidekichi Miyazaki, who set a Guinness World Record in 2015 at age 105 for sprinting 100 metres. I give him credit at that age just for being able to hear the starter's pistol.

And in 2017 Julia Hawkins, age 101 became the oldest woman ever in the USA Track and Field Outdoors Masters Championship, running 100 metres in 40.12 seconds. This was actually a disappointment as the previous year she ran the same distance in 39.62 seconds. Maybe she should get some pointers from Hidekichi Miyazaki.

Which all gets me back to Enoch. As promised. Actually I don't care about Enoch. I want to segue to a chat about eunuchs.

A South Korean historical study found that eunuchs in the royal court lived fourteen to nineteen years longer than uncastrated men. The article is called "The Upside of Castration." I find this most uncomfortable. I certainly don't share the author's optimism. If I lived in South Korea, and if I ever wanted suggestions on how to live a longer life, I certainly would not have wanted to place my healthcare into the hands of a geriatrician. I prefer other approaches, like eating my grains, fresh veggies, and fish; getting my exercise; and keeping busy. At least this route is less invasive. Gd save the King.

And so what does it take to get older? The wise man says,

Getting older is not problem. You just have to live long enough.
~ Groucho Marx

The time has come now to discuss the final chapter, after there are no more sans any things. I talk of the guy with the shroud and the sickle; the grim reaper.

Exit Stage Up

Longevity goes only so far these days. Sooner or later we, especially the boomers, have to face taxes, or should I say that other certainty. Maybe we can take some comfort from the words of emperor and philosopher Marcus Aurelius, who said, "End thy journey in content, just as an olive falls off when it is ripe, blessing nature who produced it, and thanking the tree on which it grew."

Then again, maybe that is easy to do when you're an olive. It seems we humans are afraid of the journey's destination so much that we often skirt around the *D* word, using a variety of other expressions.

Shortly after I got married, I met an insurance broker as I was in the market for life insurance. It's not that I expected imminently to *go*. It was simply just in case. I couldn't make up my mind there and then about the merits of his wares, and I asked the man to call me back the following Tuesday. The broker responded, "What if *something should happen to you meanwhile?*" I didn't catch on.

I queried, "What might happen between Thursday and next Tuesday?" Offhand, the only plans I had entailing some risk was for a haircut on Friday.

The broker replied, "You never know, *something might happen.*"

Since he was in the business of selling life insurance, I found it rather strange he wouldn't just come out and simply say, "You might *drop dead.*" Put this way it probably would have made me think. Even if I wouldn't have grabbed his life-insurance policy that Thursday, at least I would have been extra careful. I probably wouldn't have let my barber shave my throat.

Somehow the expression "something happens" doesn't sound as terminal as "death." Although I can live with that expression, I simply cannot see the media using it to connote death. Imagine how readers would react if a newspaper obituary column carried the following listing: "Henry Dingle, eighty-three years of age, at the Riverdale Hospital. Something happened to him."

I for one would be a bit concerned about poor Henry and rather curious as to what happened to him. Other readers might even call the hospital to see whether Henry was all right and to see whether they could help.

Now if, for example, the listing went on to describe where and when the funeral would take place, it would confirm our worst suspicions. We'd know for sure Henry was *no more.* Although if we were to call the funeral parlour and ask about Henry Dingle, they would just tell us Mr. Dingle is "*resting*" there.

This is a fair statement, I guess, as poor Henry would need all the rest he could get in view of the long trip ahead of him across the Stygian River to the next world, assuming, of course, there is life after something happens.

But there is also a myriad of similar expressions that make death sound less decisive or at least less final. Sometimes a person is said to *expire*. Like a Visa card: Expires September 2023. This is not as bad as it sounds. Chances are you'll get a new card in the mail in August that will tide you over until September 2026. I would certainly choose expiry over death in the hope of ultimately having my stay on earth extended, even if only for three years at a time. Meanwhile, I might join those Okinawan fishermen. From the looks of it, they don't *drop like flies*. Then again, I wonder whether they fly fish. Curious.

Most of the other expressions fall similarly into the category of words or phrases tending to show the deceased is *no longer with us*. We will hear that Henry Dingle (we may as well use Henry and not *waste* anybody else) has *passed on* or has *departed*. This trip may sometimes find Henry converted into a chattel as people might say they have *lost* Henry.

This latter term, however, connotes some measure of hope of recovery or return; as when something is lost, there is always the lost-and-found office. It may be only a small chance, but a lost Henry is more likely to be found sitting among the purses and umbrellas than a *mortified* Henry, one who so to speak had *bit the dust*.

And speaking of chances, what happens to a man if his *number is up*? This term is ideal for lottery players and fatalists. He doesn't die; his number is just up. It's as if there's some angel of death in the netherworld turning a huge drum and pulling out people's social insurance numbers.

Children have no fear calling a spade a spade. Whenever they play military games, they have no hesitation to shout, "Bang, you're dead!" I used to play these games with my French-Canadian pals in my hometown of Montreal. Whenever I was mortally wounded in combat they'd usually shout, "Bang, bang, *tu es finis.*" They declared me to be finished, like a hard-boiled egg.

And once someone, say Henry again, does *pop off* (I can live with that one too), he is known as the *late* Henry. This expression, in my opinion, adds insult to injury, especially if ascribed to an individual who was usually punctual all his life. How could he possibly be on time now when he has no way of getting to where he's expected? Why call him late? It's not his fault he *kicked the bucket.*

There's absolutely no justification in calling the individual late once he's gone *belly up.* Late people still eventually do show up. But Henry isn't coming back unless he's got those strange powers Patrick Swayze had in the movie *Ghost.* He hung around for a while it seems, and it did not look like he had *given up the ghost.*

On the brighter side of things, at least there's overwhelming proof that there is life after death. If there wasn't, people would never go around saying Henry has *gone to meet his maker.*

More about life after death to follow. First, the funeral.

The Funeral

I find it disturbing to see those ads for planning a funeral in advance. In my humble view, funeral arrangements should take place after the deceased you know what. OK, dies.

It's not like after Henry dies there will be a run on the services of undertakers and Henry will not be buried. I have never heard of funeral directors talking of a full house sellout. There is always room for one more. Nor is it like a shortage of tickets to a Leafs game. I have never heard of scalper undertakers.

And speaking of funeral directors, I wonder whether some large mega retailers like Walmart will one day go into the undertaking business. They already have law offices on site where in-house lawyers perform legal services, including wills. It's only a short step further after the will comes into play. One problem I see is that the star of the show, namely the deceased, does not get to enjoy the pleasure of crossing paths with the Walmart greeter.

Or might another giant like Costco expand its services in this high-demand market? Might be a neat fit. Costco is known to have these stations where they hand out samples (pre-COVID of course). I'm not sure any of the customers would care for this aspect. I know I'd sooner go for a cracker and some aged Cheddar.

Also, Costco generally sells items in bulk or larger sizes and quantities. I suppose this might work if the deal is good, and two lovers would consider buying two coffins. After all, they sell olive oil in quantities of a two-pack. (I'm tempted to say a bit more about Marcus Aurelius's olive now, but I'll resist the temptation.)

And what is most exceptional at Costco is their generous refund policy, no questions asked. I haven't seen it yet, but what if one day scientists discover a way to bring back the dead. You never know. In that case, just stand in that return merchandise line and return those items. The Costco clerk might ask if there's anything wrong with them. Just say something like, "Not really. Henry just came back." While you're there you can also ask them to reinstate his membership.

And I can certainly see Amazon enter the undertaking industry. One-stop shop. Just give them a call and a drone comes over and picks up Henry. And to keep an eye on all the preparations and activities they'll even give you a tracking number.

Hey, is any of this far-fetched? Remember what Charles Duell said in 1901 about everything that can be invented has already been invented. We must keep an open mind.

As part of the deal they can throw in a few condolences. Which brings me to eulogies.

Although they are an important aspect of the death ceremony, I find some of the stock comments useless and meaningless to the deceased and those listening.

One such common eulogy I have already mentioned is, "He lived life to the fullest." What exactly does that mean? He was up 24/7? Never spent time sleeping? Or did he not waste time? In my view he was disqualified from living life to the fullest if he spent more than two minutes scrolling through Facebook reading about how Amanda messed up her inaugural attempt to bake an upside-down banana cake.

You can live life to the fullest only if you're perfect, and even then, as one of my favourite philosophers, Yogi Berra, used to say, "If the world were perfect, it wouldn't be."

Another phrase that bugs me is, "He died like he lived." When I hear this one, all I can think about is some criminal or criminals, like Bonnie and Clyde. Nobody dies like they lived, not even Al Capone. He died of heart failure. I doubt many people will agree that Al Capone displayed much of a heart while he lived in Chicago plying his trade.

The expression that we hear very often and that is most often not applicable is, "He had a sense of humour that was infectious." Though I believe that most of us have a sense of humour, most people as they grow up stifle and muzzle it for many reasons, including the mythological view that humour is not serious.

I once went to a funeral service for a judge. If he had a sense of humour, he certainly didn't display it in court. On a good day he was at best a hanging judge. Fortunately, capital punishment was off the books during his time on the bench. Maybe had it still been around, he would have displayed some of that infectious sense of humour, perhaps saying during a sentencing, "On July 11th, you will be taken to the gallows where you will be introduced to the hangman. I believe his name is Herman."

To him, Shakespeare's words of "when mercy seasons justice" had no meaning. He was rough and rude with clients, witnesses, and lawyers alike.

Then again what could anyone have said about this judge? How about, "It will be difficult to get along without Justice Gilbert Ludlow, but starting this afternoon, we shall all give it a good try"?

That of course was not his real name. I will not divulge it in the event that he just might return. I'd sure hate to bump into him at Costco.

When we learn that somebody died, the first question often is, "How old was he?" If it's a child, the reaction is one of tragedy. If it's a middle-aged person, you'll often hear, "Oh my. He was a father of four." If it's someone past seventy, you'll get, "At least he lived life to the fullest. He'll be sorely missed." I'm sure he will be. Sorely that is.

I doubt most people think of themselves in these terms, and if asked the question before they kick off, whether they would agree. Most folks if asked would say something like, "Live life to the fullest? Are you kidding? I wasted too much time and effort cheering on those hapless Toronto Blue Jays."

And what do you say when a really old person dies? Like I said earlier, I had the pleasure of meeting Ben Sherman who died at age 105. After I heard the news, I uttered, "Hey, I recently shook his hand." I felt a sense of empowerment, as if shaking the hand of a centenarian transmits longevity.

But is death the end of the line?

Where There's a Will

I have little. I owe much. The rest I leave to the poor.
~ François Rabelais

In my forty-plus years of practice I prepared some wills for clients. Not many. Firstly, it wasn't my specialty, and more important, I didn't like doing wills as they reminded me of where this was all going. I didn't like the fact that the testator signing it will not be the last person to ever see it.

I can say most folks shared my sentiments and hated discussing it more than they had to. I got the feeling the experience was akin to that proverbial root canal, although the dentist charges a lot more for the pain he causes.

I did get some cute comments from clients, such as, "Now that I've done my will I probably won't die." Or "Remember, when I go I want a regular burial in a cemetery. Remind my cheapskate son that I don't want to be cremated." A great one a client said was, "I hope I don't have to see you too soon again about this after it's over." He was not a pleasant fellow and if after he died, he was going where I thought he was going eventually, I certainly didn't want to meet him there.

Which brings me to ...

Life After Death. Is There Any?

The short answer is "sort of." You go from being Henry Dingle to the Estate of Henry Dingle. And if there's money there, your relatives will find you no problem. And if they don't like your will, they'll fight among themselves and try to convince a judge that this wasn't really what you wanted, or rather what you willed. The grouches will plead that when you did your will your mind really wasn't all there. You were *non compos mentis*, or mentally incompetent, or as they say in legal lingo, you weren't playing with a full deck.

Or they may plead that the will is invalid as the lucky beneficiary exerted undue influence over you, or as they say in legal lingo, twisted your arm. Chances are he or she was the one who brought the testator to the lawyer's office to start with. Ah huh! Guilty.

And so while the family and other beneficiaries or wannabe beneficiaries sort it out, or perhaps duke it out, the short answer is, there is life after death. As we all know, the deceased is watching all of this wrangling over what is or was his, and is at times likely rolling in his grave.

But does he go anywhere after all of this rolling. Is there a soul or spirit that indeed takes a voyage now that the body is no more?

I can say that boomers are now the vanguard, age-wise, of wherever this is going given that we are some of the dwindling few who still remember some twentieth-century icons, such as John F. Kennedy, Golda Meir, and Yogi Bear. We're getting there.

Who knows indeed? Firstly, nobody has ever returned from wherever they might be going. We have yet to see a broadcast on *Fox News* saying, "Our next guest is William Langley, who died last month and who has returned to tell us about the other world. If you think we have problems with global warming, wait till you hear from Bill."

Which of course brings us to, pardon the expression, hell. We won't spend too much time here. Promise. As Sir Winston Churchill once said, "If you're going through hell, keep moving."

Is there a place like hell? I have other questions. If there is a hell, is it really hot? And do they announce the temperatures in Celsius or Fahrenheit. If Celsius, I know this would drive the American guests looney. If they'd hear today's temperature is forty-five degrees, they'd rush to put on their down-filled coats. At least we Canadians would enjoy watching them.

Most important question: If hell is hot, can you upgrade to an air-conditioned room? Just asking. I note there is a dearth of information about the climate in paradise. I'm still waiting for some announcement on this issue, maybe on the Weather Channel?

And is there a devil there? If so, does he carry a trident, wear a cape, and have horns? I doubt even William Langley can tell us. Maybe he went to heaven. And if he did, does that place look like "paradise"? And if so, does paradise look anything like the Garden of Eden? That doesn't sound too bad, as long as you remember to watch your selection of produce.

Another vital question is, who decides where you go? St. Peter? If so, I have a number of questions:

1. Who is this guy after all? Who made him the gatekeeper? Face it, he's not like Moses, who got word of his position via that burning bush.

2. Did he apply for the job by submitting his resumé? "Experienced. Did gatekeeping before as a doctor's secretary. Was very nasty. Didn't put anybody through to the doctor."

3. How old is this guy now? Is he a millennial? That would not be good—for us boomers. I have a good idea of which door he'll be sending us through.

4. Is he tech-equipped? There's lots of business these days. It would not surprise me if he is holding an iPad. I guess this would presuppose the netherworld has Wi-Fi.

5. How does he make his decisions as to who goes where? Where does he get his pertinent info? If my hunch in the previous

question is spot on, he probably just gets it from the likes of Siri. Or Alexa. Hell!

6. Does he get paid? If so, I wonder what he would earn. The minimum wage in Ontario is $15/hour. No clue what it might be upstairs.

7. What are his hours? Eight hours/day? Does he get breaks? Actually, I can visualize a sign at the gate reading, "Back in ten minutes. Stay cool"

8. Does he get vacation time off? If so, where does he go? I wouldn't suggest a Caribbean cruise. To me all islands look alike. Seen one, seen them all.

9. If he does go on vacation, who replaces him? Is it anything like when a doctor is away? Is the gate manned by a locum? "Good day. St. Peter is away this week. My name is St. Sylvester. I'll be your gatekeeper. Be with you shortly. Just sign in on that iPad.

10. What is his job description? Is he expected to do non-gate-keeping tasks, such as making coffee?

11. Are there benefits linked to his job? I'm sure he gets a uniform. What about a pension?

12. Being a lawyer, I must ask if his decision is final, or can it be appealed? Then again, being a lawyer and given the reputation our profession sometimes has, I have concerns about any biases such an appeal tribunal might have.

I'm certain many of us boomers must be thinking about these issues. As those bank, government, or utility company voicemails say, "We're busy helping other clients. You're in the queue."

CHAPTER ELEVEN

It's All a Theatre of Sorts. Isn't It?

I started out discussing Shakespeare's seven stages of man. I agree that the very end did not look too promising, *but* we boomers are basically OK. Why? Because nowhere does Shakespeare ascribe numbers to the stages. He may talk about the fat-bellied judge, but how old is this guy? The bard does not say anything at all about the magic of age sixty-five. Nor does he talk about retirement. He doesn't say, "Happy sixty-fifth birthday. Give the guy in the pantaloons a gold watch." Or in his days, maybe just another pair of those pantaloons.

One label just does not fit all. True, our physical status takes a bit of a hit. But isn't that all part of the human condition, young and old alike? Let us not forget the world-class kiddie hospital in Toronto called "The Hospital for Sick Children." At least at our age we won't trouble the healthcare system with kiddie problems such as chicken pox, measles, or swallowed nickels.

There are brilliant boomer players still on that stage, from presidents to prime ministers, to physicians to comedians plying their callings.

As I said earlier, we boomers have something the younger gang doesn't have experience in. We are adept at the three *R*s. We can still do multiplication and division in case our iPhone's battery crashes. And we can still read an article where there is no heads-up warning saying, "Note, seven-minute read. Have your bottle of spring water ready."

And we can even write in cursive. Yes, that word is still in the English dictionary. We don't rush onto Facebook and post a panicky "OMG."

Most important is that we appreciate a sense of humour. (OK, humor for our friends south of the border). We've had the privilege of listening and watching the works of icons such as Bob Hope, Mel Brooks, and Woody Allen. And Carl Reiner, RIP. Aren't we grateful these old men didn't slow down at age sixty-five?

The younger generations, unfortunately, have had their appreciation of humour compromised big time. Comedian Jerry Seinfeld generally avoids appearances before college crowds, noting that they are too sensitive, jumping to label every joke racist or sexist or otherwise prejudicial. And as I write, Jerome Allen Seinfeld is sixty-seven years of age.

Just look at the classical joke genres and tell me if the joker would run into trouble with the politically correct police.

1. Knock Knock? Who's there? No way José. "No way José" is not part of the joke. I am simply saying that you cannot use this knock knock formula anymore as it likely violates rights to privacy. Nowadays you simply do not dare do that. After all, we have never had as much privacy as we have now. Privacy is sacrosanct. Nobody has a clue what we are doing on our computers. Furthermore, the term "Knock" evokes an image of violence. You cannot hit anything, let alone a door. Some folks may feel offended and they'll have to find a safe room. Maybe that room is behind that door you're knocking on. Who knows?

2. An Englishman, a Frenchman, and a German enter a bar. I don't care what any of them order at the bar. Any way you pour it, some people will rule it out as being racist. I can only imagine there will be a cute punchline after the Englishman orders his scotch, the Frenchman his Champaign, and the German his beer. But I will not venture a guess what the punchline will be. Verboten.

3. A close cousin to this genre is "There is a priest, a minister, and a rabbi." Try one of these jokes in places such as some university campuses and you risk getting drawn and quartered. Actually, there is a double risk: one for including these three religious representatives and possibly another for failing to include reps of other religions. And I don't even know where agnostics and atheists fall into the picture. The human rights tribunals would have a feast on you.

4. How about the hyperbole joke, such as "It's so hot that …" Don't dare touch this one with a ten-foot spatula. If you do, you will be making light of climate change. No weather is funny. Pass.

5. Why did the chicken cross the road? Uh huh—animal rights. Ask that one again and you may as well invite PETA to converge on your house with torches and pitchforks.

6. And don't ask what you get when you cross an elephant with a jar of peanut butter. Triple no-no. In addition to (1) knocking animals—sorry, make that assailing animals, you are (2) messing with genetically modified organisms, and (3) offending the allergy associations given that there is a plague of people allergic to peanuts. FYI, I might get some slack cut on that one; one of my sons and granddaughters are in that club. Actually,

I know the answer to that joke but I'm not talking. Google it. Given your secure privacy status, nobody will know.

7. And likely the shortest joke in the English language, the iconic joke, the signature joke of the "King of the One Liners," Henny Youngman, is definitely taboo. I am talking, of course, of "Take my wife, please." Now was the legendary comedian being sexist or disrespectful to his wife? You tell me. Did you know the two were happily married for sixty years? Just maybe the humour helped cement a marital union of the type you rarely find today.

Can the world lighten up a bit? As legendary humourist Erma Bombeck once said, "When humour goes, there goes civilization." Anybody listening? We boomers are. And our humour is contributing to the flame of civilization.

Using our sense of humour is vital. We have the ability and the luxury to see life's foibles through humour lenses (not bifocals). We all have one. People my vintage are living in a different world than we grew up in. There is technology to figure out. Perpetual voicemail pain, Siri, robots. Let's laugh whenever we get stuck trying to navigate a website or email thread or word-processing task without the help of our children, or rather, grandchildren. And speaking of the kids, we may as well smile as we listen to their peculiar vocabulary. Whatever.

Let's see the humour in smart driverless cars. I just hope that while on the highway they'll be smart enough to pull over when nature calls—at one of those service stops.

Are we old? We are not young. Are we aging? Yes, all of us one way or another. Even the millennials and the Zs were younger when you started reading that seven-minute read.

Can we do something about it? Yes, the younger people more so. Let me share the wise words of Canadian quintessential humourist Stephen Leacock:

> How strange it is, our little procession of life! The child says, "When I am a big boy." But what is that? The big boy says, "When I grow up." And then, grown up, he says, "When I get married." But to be married, what is that after all? The thought changes to "When I'm able to retire." And then, when retirement comes, he looks back over the landscape traversed; a cold wind seems to sweep over it; somehow he has missed it all, and it is gone. Life, we learn too late, is in the living, in the tissue of every day and hour.

That scenario doesn't sound too promising. But do we have to follow this script? I don't think so. We can't all run those marathons, but as long as we're still on that stage, how about we behave and give a dynamite performance.

Not making an exit at this time. To aging better. Cheers.